MICHAEL TAYLOR
INTERIOR DESIGN

Michael Taylor

Michael Taylor in his office at Sea Cliff, 1984.

MICHAEL TAYLOR
INTERIOR DESIGN

STEPHEN M. SALNY

FOREWORD BY ROSE TARLOW

W. W. NORTON & COMPANY

New York • London

To

JUNE AND ALAN SALNY

My loving and supportive parents who always see to it
that I have everything I need to accomplish my goals.

Copyright (c) 2008 by Stephen M. Salny

Printed in Singapore
First Edition

For information about permission to reproduce
selections from this book, write to Permissions,
W. W. Norton & Company, Inc., 500 Fifth Avenue
New York, NY 10110

For information about special discounts for bulk purchases,
please contact W. W. Norton Special Sales at
specialsales@wwnorton.com or 800-233-4830

Manufacturing by KHL Singapore
Book design by Abigail Sturges
Production manager: Leeann Graham

Library of Congress Cataloging-in-Publication Data

Salny, Stephen M.
Michael Taylor : interior design / Stephen M. Salny ;
foreword by Rose Tarlow. — 1st ed.
p. cm.
Includes bibliographical references and index.
ISBN 978-0-393-73235-1 (hardcover)
1. Taylor, Michael, 1927-1986. 2. Interior decoration—United
States—History—20th century. I. Title.
NK2004.3.T39S25 2008
747.092—dc22

                                    2008013378

W. W. Norton & Company, Inc., 500 Fifth Avenue,
New York, N.Y. 10110
www.wwnorton.com

W. W. Norton & Company Ltd., Castle House, 75/76 Wells Street,
London W1T 3QT

0 9 8 7 6 5 4 3 2 1

Page 1 Portrait of Michael Taylor by Pedro Leitao, pencil
and colored pencil on paper, Lisbon, Portugal, 1964.

CONTENTS

FOREWORD

[signature: Rose Tarlow]

ROSE TARLOW

We met in January 1976, in the middle of the street, on Melrose Place. I was crossing over to inspect the new shop directly across from me, and Michael Taylor was on his way over to introduce himself to me, the only other newcomer on the block. It was then that we discovered we both were celebrating our individual birthdays as well as opening new shops. From that day forward, we continually compared the many astrological similarities that influenced our daily lives and began a friendship that would enrich my life and affect my design aesthetic for all time.

It was the mid-1970s, when Melrose Place was lined on both sides by shops that had built impressive reputations over many years. Each one was filled with the finest antique furniture and objects. I was thrilled to have the privilege of having an antique shop on Melrose Place. People came from all over to shop on our street. Because it was such a hot spot, the location would attract the larger-than-life magic man from San Francisco.

Michael Taylor brought with him a completely new vision; I doubt that there were twenty objects in his sparkling, light-filled space. In complete contrast to my "chock-full of everything under the sun" shop, Taylor, Wilson and House had rough stone floors, tall palms, white powdery plaster walls, bleached wood furniture, huge raw crystals, and primitive Mayan art brought back from Peru, where Michael had just spent many months searching for treasures. The objects and the furniture, like Michael himself, were gorgeous and gigantic. The exceptional, overscaled furniture—which we now take for granted as uniquely Californian—was then extremely unusual. I like to think that, whatever Michael was doing in San Francisco at the time, the "California Look" was born in that shop on Melrose Place. This genius of a man gave us an extraordinary gift: an identity we could call our very own.

I have always compared Michael's impact on design to Jackson Pollock's on art. Pollock, with his childlike splashes of paint on canvas in such a seemingly simplistic form, created a new way of seeing. With such naïve innovations, he made a profound statement and marked a turning point in American art. Michael Taylor made just such a contribution to the world of interiors. He incorporated into his work the most common and primitive elements of nature: straw carpets, ancient clay pottery, Indian baskets and artifacts, tree stump tables and beds, rocks and trees—an inexhaustible storehouse of ready-made creations that had been exclusive to tribal living for centuries.

I believe the eye is educated by everything it sees. Once, when Michael and I were standing in a garden outdoors, I pointed to a tree and said, in an effort to impress him with my discerning eye, "That is truly an ugly tree!" He turned, stared down at me with that lofty imperial look of his, and announced, "There are no ugly trees." As he had in his shop, he brought into our living rooms the outdoors, nature, and everything under the sun. He brought in the sun, as well, through skylights and open spaces. Simple natural treasures, available to everybody, became the essential elements of Michael Taylor's design, which changed California's, and the world's, approach to interior space.

Michael had two very different expressions of decorating, both totally unique—as you will see in this comprehensive study of his work. One was his "traditional rooms" style; the other was what I have named his "sticks-and-stones" style, of which he was the pioneer.

I have been enormously influenced by these traditional rooms throughout the years, and viewing them again in this excellent historical retrospective, they still have the power to stir my emotions. It is not only the juxtaposition of furniture and special objects but also the sum of all his magic: his controlled use of color, light, and multiple textures and surfaces that combine to create an experience of irreproachable beauty that to this day reminds me of just how influential his body of work really was.

Michael's interiors were as bold as they were brilliant. Rules never applied to Michael in design or in life. He created the way he wanted to live and he created his own design vocabulary. In one of our many long phone conversations, he described to me a Victorian house in San Francisco he was working on. I pleaded with him to let me see it. It was an unbelievable experience. Who but Michael would dare to cover all the walls of a living room in white Chinese wallpaper and then fill the room with white painted Victorian furniture covered in English country chintz? Never mind that antique Chinese paper never had a white background and that heavy, dark, classic Victorian furniture was never painted white. Then, to top off this confection, he covered all the furniture in the room in fabric with pink cabbage roses! Every rule of design was torn to shreds. I still wonder at the colossal confidence it took to even conceive of such a preposterous combination.

MICHAEL TAYLOR

Antiques • *Interior Design*

MICHAEL TAYLOR
Antiques . *Interior Design*

9 Twenty-Fifth Avenue North ● San Francisco, CA 94121 ● (415) 668-7668

9 Twenty-Fifth Avenue North • San Francisco, California 94121 • (415) 668-7668

Michael Taylor, Inc. business card, Sea Cliff; letterhead, Sutter Street.

I treasured Michael's friendship; he was enormous fun to be with. However, when he visited my shop I was both thrilled and terrified. He was extremely opinionated. He loved giving me ideas about what I should be doing or buying . . . or how I could improve my sales staff . . . or how I could win lovers and influence clients. He was full of advice and criticism, and of course all these helpful hints were delivered in his often-grandiose condescending manner. Once I had an antique screen in my shop in which he showed some vague interest but dismissed it; some weeks later he remembered and desired it. When I told him it was sold, he did not speak to me for six months. To apologize, I sent him a chartreuse cable-knit cashmere sweater from one of his favorite sweater designers, Andre Oliver. He forgave me but mentioned that he already had several in that color. Another time I sent him a gold Tiffany pen. He already had ten. On the rare occasion when he wanted to make up with me, he sent me a sterling silver 9-by-12-inch picture frame holding a big black-and-white glossy photo of himself.

Michael knew he was a star and was superbly confident in this persona. Humility was not a gene he possessed. He had a difficult time denying himself anything. As a modern Louis XIV incarnate, he entertained and lived majestically. Michael was grander than any of his clients, which was both his weakness and uniqueness. Dinner was served formally on wonderful agate plates with magnificent silver and the most glorious table accessories. He adored good food and beautiful clothes, and he always rented a Rolls Royce even if he was just in town for the day. He took great pride in his wardrobe and would point out what great new purchase he was sporting. It could be his new alligator Bennisson loafers, of which he had shelves full. Or his new leather jacket, one of hundreds. He was notorious for having little control or even a slight show of healthy remorse over his excessive acquisitiveness. One day he came into my shop with his client and great friend Jimmie Wilson. When Michael could not cajole Jimmie into buying an outrageously costly rock-crystal chandelier, he turned and said, "Jimmie, if you don't buy it, then lend me the money to buy it for myself!"

Often Michael would telephone me just before dinner and keep me on the phone for ages. I remember exhaustingly trying to entertain him with some amusing tale of the day. I would dread these calls; the pressure was daunting trying to keep this intimidating person, who was easily bored, sufficiently amused that he would keep calling. One day I became fed up with hearing myself talk without any feedback, and I decided to see just how long it would take for him to notice I had not uttered a word. I timed 14 minutes without either of us even breathing loudly! Years later, when a few of his friends and I were reminiscing about our friendships with Michael, I relayed the history of these weird one-sided conversations and was laughingly informed that Michael called all his friends at that time of day while watching his favorite television show, "Jeopardy."

The last time Michael and I visited together was on one of his few trips to Los Angeles. It was a very special evening because I had him all to myself, which was a rare occurrence as he usually traveled in the company of others. Just before dinner, we drove in his convertible Rolls to look at the new house I had recently purchased and was planning to renovate for myself. I was excited to show him my first real project. We walked around, and I explained what I intended to do. He listened, said nothing, then at dinner looked me in the eye and said, "tear it down." I gasped, argued, and declined to accept his suggestion. This was sadly our last visit. The next Michael moment I had was when I attended his funeral in San Francisco. After the funeral, I returned to Los Angeles with a feeling of monumental loss. The next day I went to my job site, which was by then in full-swing renovation. I took my contractor aside and said, "Tear it down." I know it sounds a bit dramatic, but I guess in my heart I always knew that, as usual, Michael was right. I love my house as it is now, and I only wish he were here to criticize it. I don't have my friend anymore, but I do have many bittersweet memories, some lovely mementos, and, best of all, his handsome, movie-star, black-and-white, glossy photograph in its sterling-silver frame, looking at me. I am quite sure he is probably agreeing with me that he was and still is the very best of the best.

AN OVERVIEW

At six-foot-four and 240 pounds, interior decorator/designer Michael Taylor resembled a football player (which he had been briefly) or, with his rugged handsomeness, a movie actor (a career that he had considered). His parents, Earnest and Grace Taylor, had wanted him to study medicine, and he served as a paramedic in the U.S. Navy during World War II. The experience soured him on becoming a physician, and when the war was over he focused on his childhood passion: design and the discovery and collecting of beautiful objects. Taylor's maternal grandmother, Nelly Peck, had instilled in him a love of natural beauty. Together, he and his grandmother regularly explored beaches and redwood forests and "looked at the beauty of shells, tree stumps, rocks, and flowers—into the beauty of things that cost nothing." His ascent in the world of design was rapid: within a decade of leaving the navy he became internationally known. By the time of his death, he would be revered as one of the most innovative, imitated, and internationally respected design icons of the twentieth century.

Taylor's most notable contribution to interior design was the "California Look," the revolutionary design aesthetic that he pioneered during the early 1970s. Taylor brought the outdoors inside with neutral palettes, natural light, large-scale furniture, and organic elements, especially stone, slate, wicker, and plants. His interiors expressed his love and appreciation of California and the outdoors. They were casual, comfortable, uncomplicated, and free of clutter.

Earnest Charles Taylor (he later changed his name to Michael because it was sexy and youthful) was born in Modesto, California, in 1927. In 1933 his family moved to Santa Rosa. In 1944 he dropped out of high school to enter the navy, serving in southern California and in Brooklyn, New York. After receiving his discharge in 1946, Taylor moved to San Francisco where, in 1947, he began study at the internationally acclaimed Rudolph Schaeffer School of Design. Schaeffer "was in the forefront of art education in the perception and use of colors." Taylor recalled in a 1973 *California Living* magazine article that Schaeffer was a gifted instructor who "enlightened" me, "opening my eyes to vistas I wasn't aware of. He made me conscious of possibilities." Taylor absorbed from Schaeffer what Schaeffer called "the secrets of color." Taylor's amazing sense of light and how it could be used were among his greatest talents. Schaeffer's instruction would trigger Taylor's fascination with white, which Taylor believed was "the most efficient

color for capturing both natural and man-made light." The use of white, which was unfashionable at the time, would become one of Taylor's most recognizable signatures.

Taylor's respect and appreciation for his mentor was returned. Schaeffer referred to Taylor as "his dear Michael," whose work was "wild, but extremely creative" and as exciting as "fireworks" that were "going off all the time." Schaeffer influenced the course of Taylor's career by recommending him to a respected San Francisco fabric dealer, Frederick Bruns, who hired Taylor as a showroom assistant in mid-1947. Taylor never looked back. Over the next five years, he moved from Bruns's showroom to work as an assistant to Archibald Taylor (no relation), the leading San Francisco interior designer. From Archibald Taylor's office, where Taylor was employed for three years—primarily as an errand boy, which exposed him to a plenitude of beautiful houses decorated by his employer—he moved to the respected decorating department at the Oakland, California branch of Breuner's, the largest chain of home furnishings stores in the country. Robert and Vale Kasper, owners of a prominent San Francisco furniture–interior design firm and design pioneers themselves, heard about Taylor's revolutionary and unorthodox taste, which simplified interiors and combined contemporary and traditional furniture. Based on his successful initiation and execution of custom designs at Breuner's—which was rare at the time—the Kaspers invited Taylor to join their employ.

At the Kasper firm Taylor nurtured his relationships with women who were to become pivotal to his career. Taylor already knew Irma Schlesinger slightly, as he was a good friend of her daughter, Nan Schlesinger. Through Nan, Taylor orchestrated a visit to the Schlesingers' modernist Gardner Dailey house in Pacific Heights, where he scrutinized the work of another woman who would dramatically influence his career: the renowned decorator Frances Elkins (1888–1953). Elkins was in the process of fine-tuning the Schlesingers' interiors that she had decorated for an April 1952 *Vogue* magazine feature shoot entitled "San Francisco House." Taylor came to idolize Elkins, and the legendary interior designer greatly influenced his work. Taylor saw himself as Elkins's greatest disciple, and he believed completely in her genius: "She certainly was one of the guiding forces in the whole development of what is the American style today." His adoration would be repaid. One day Elkins sought Taylor out in the Kaspers' store to tell him personally how impressed she was with

MAY

House & Garden

75¢

REMODELING:
your space redesigned • redecorated • rejuvenated
• face-lifting for bathrooms
DECORATING:
big effects on little money • furniture finds under $44

COOK BOOK:
how to make 31 kinds of quiche

House & Garden magazine, May 1968. Benoist Commission,
Los Gatos, California.

the design work that he had done in the storefront windows. It was an early triumph.

Another admirer of Taylor's from this period at the Kaspers was Kay Benoist, whose husband Louis owned Almaden Vineyards in northern California. Attracted by Taylor's work, the couple eventually hired him. Over the next thirty-five years Taylor would decorate nine houses, two yachts, and an airplane for them. The Benoists and Taylor eventually became close personal friends.

While working at the Kasper firm, Taylor also met Frances Mihailoff, a woman twenty-six years his senior who was also an interior designer in the firm. Mihailoff recognized in Taylor visionary taste, and she suggested that they go out on their own. In 1952 they established their own interior design firm, Taylor and Mihailoff, at 453 Post Street, on the ground floor of the St. Francis Hotel.

Taylor and Mihailoff was an immediate success. The firm received numerous commissions from the San Francisco elite. In 1953 alone, *House Beautiful* magazine featured Taylor and Mihailoff's work on its covers three separate times: in February, July, and October. The October cover featured a living room with a sleek low-set armless sofa upholstered in crisp white hand-woven Italian linen. The editors proclaimed that the sofa represented "a new look in furniture." The two decorators were the epitome of "the new, rich look now entering our homes." This recognition only intensified the firm's acclaim. Their work represented the "graceful merging of design influence," ending the battle between modern and traditional styles.

By 1954, the success and rapid growth of Taylor and Mihailoff had enabled the two partners to separate and establish businesses on their own. Mihailoff moved to 540 Sutter Street. Taylor purchased Mihailoff's interest in the business with a loan from San Francisco industrialist Ralph K. Davies and remained at the Post Street shop for two years until he found a new space that would signal his extraordinary talent and swift success. It would both showcase his soon-to-be signature overscaled designs and reflect his intimidating and intensely driven persona.

Taylor's new shop was located at 556 Sutter Street in an L-shaped, white stucco building owned by Elizabeth Arden. The building also housed Arden's salon, whose contemporary and understated design was justifiably famous. Arden enthusiastically embraced Taylor because they shared the same clientele. Arden also became Taylor's client. One day she walked into his shop and purchased all his major room designs of furniture and accessories, which she then had flown to Florida. She also hired Taylor to design and decorate the octagonal pavilion that crowned her four-story spa and salon on Sutter Street. This was the place where Arden's patrons completed their coiffure under a uniformly lined bank of hair dryers. Taylor created an interior gazebo with walls of creamy-white treillage interspersed with tall

Right: Taylor & Mihailoff storefront, 453 Post Street.

Below: Taylor & Mihailoff business card.

TAYLOR/MIHAILOFF
453 Post Street San Francisco 2, EXbrook 2-7590
Frances Mihailoff A.I.D. Michael Taylor

arched windows. An umbrella of brightly striped fabric draped the pavilion ceiling.

The entrance to Elizabeth Arden was located on the east side of the building, set back from Sutter Street by an iron-gated courtyard with a manicured lawn and a profusion of white rose standards. The imposing gate, which was always attended by a pair of liveried doormen in custom khaki uniforms and flat-topped bill hats, opened onto a brick walkway that led to Arden's signature brilliant-red lacquered front door.

In addition to Elizabeth Arden's "institution," the 500 block of Sutter Street was lined with specialty shops that catered to San Francisco's carriage trade. Nelly Gaffney, a fashionable women's dress shop, was located nearby on the corner of Sutter and Mason Streets. Women also gathered at the Francisca Club, an exclusive women's organization located across the street from the dress shop. The Medico-Dental building, which was nearby on Post Street, drew a perpetual corps of women bringing their children for doctors' appointments. Michael Taylor, Inc., was located on the west side of Arden's building, on the ground floor. It quickly became a regular and eagerly anticipated destination for this elite and au courant circle of women, their families, and their friends.

Another notable neighbor on the block, next door to Nelly Gaffney, was Williams-Sonoma. Chuck Williams, who founded the specialty kitchenware store in 1956 in the Napa Valley and moved to San Francisco in 1958 to be nearer his principal clientele, was at the forefront of retailing in the United States. He introduced quality French cookware to Americans, changing the way they cooked at home. Taylor frequented Williams's store and, like the rest of America, was drawn to its unique look. He was especially taken with Williams's imported oyster baskets. The graduated baskets, shipped at great expense to San Francisco in nests of five, were originally used to transport oysters from the coast of France to Paris. Their heavy natural weave appealed to Taylor.

Taylor believed that nature was man's best friend, and his liberal and progressive use of organic elements in his refreshingly relaxed, comfortable, and unconventional interiors substantiated this philosophy. Taylor found Williams's oyster baskets at once completely new and yet deeply familiar. They had a profound effect on him. He began to use them as vessels for towering plants and trees—fishtail palms, ficus, and Zimmer linden—creating a look that became fundamental to Michael Taylor interiors. Taylor, who believed that plants prevent "a room from feeling over-decorated," "soften the light," and "help a room breathe and feel alive," initiated "the plant in a basket craze" with Williams's baskets. Taylor continued to popularize this trend by zealously cornering the steady supply of woven-rattan Philippine market baskets imported by the New Manila Importing Company in San Francisco. Thus Chuck Williams's baskets helped to launch the "California Look."

Michael Taylor, Inc., fronted Sutter Street and was colossal. Although Taylor only had eight hundred dollars in the bank at the time that he committed himself to the new space, he spent extravagant amounts of money (assisted by more loans from clients) on the renovation, especially of the new storefront, whose charismatic design was intended to both mesmerize and intimidate the passersby.

Taylor's shop was dazzling and dramatically revolutionary. He opened up the space considerably, installing a pair of twenty-foot-tall windows that were the largest single pieces of plate glass in San Francisco at the time. They balanced a set of white wooden double doors,

Michael Taylor Inc. storefront, 556 Sutter Street.

twelve feet tall, three feet wide, and four inches thick, that opened and closed effortlessly. Taylor, with his penchant for exacting precision and perfection, would not have accepted them any other way. The interior glowed with Taylor's specially formulated "Michael Taylor White" on the walls and ceiling. (Never pure white, "Michael Taylor White" was a mixture of warm colors with a beige tone.) The flooring was pure-white, twelve-inch-square, Corlon vinyl tile. He partitioned the shop into four equal-sized compartments that opened to a center aisle running from the front door to a bare twelve-foot-tall oak tree anchored in a bed of gray river rock at the back of the shop. Three of the compartments were used for rotating room setups. The fourth contained a shelf-lined boutique stocked with accessories for sale. Taylor aligned the principal setups with the storefront windows, allowing his trailblazing designs full-time exposure.

One of Taylor's first setups was prominently underscored in *Vogue's* 1956 "Fashions in Living" feature advising its readership on a "fresh way to keep a white bedroom fresh." Taylor's memorable room, which remains legendary to this day, used a pickled-pine and painted Syrie Maugham Regency canopy bed, which served to anchor the all-white room. Taylor greatly admired Maugham (1879–1955), the prominent English interior designer who pioneered white interiors and popularized the design of these beds (along with Frances Elkins). Typically, their front posts were carved and painted to resemble clustered bamboo. Taylor also liked the scalloped wood crown cornice, which injected a touch of the Far East into the decor. The opaque Fortisan bedspread, skirt, and hangings also contributed an ethereal quality to the setup.

Taylor accented the all-white bedroom with varied shades of green. The pickled-pine English chinoiserie bench fronting the bed was cushioned with a green bird-and-leaf jacquard weave, and the pair of skirted spun-rayon Syrie Maugham fireside armchairs had medium-green buttons and bowties. He also arranged the bedroom with lush plants and fresh flowers. The plaster lamps in the style of Alberto Giacometti (1902–1985) flanking the fireplace echoed Frances Elkins's avant-garde style of decorating.

Although Taylor's rooms were known for their neutral palette, Taylor always "advocated a strong secondary color and repetitive use of printed fabrics for 'a certain purity' and a bold unified effect." He also clarified that "There is a tremendous amount of color in my rooms, but there are not *many* colors."

Taylor's shop contained a spacious loft upstairs and a set of back quarters that were concealed from public view. An open flight of steps,

"Syrie Maugham" bedroom, Michael Taylor Inc, Sutter Street, 1956.

House & Garden magazine, February 1957.

paved in white Corlon vinyl, led from the right rear corner of the ground floor upstairs to the loft. Although Taylor occasionally arranged setups in the loft, he used this mezzanine level primarily for storage. More often than not, it would be packed with the treasures, furniture, accessories, and endless bolts of fabric he obtained on his extravagant shopping marathons. These shopping marathons were legendary. When Taylor entered a shop, he always paused at its threshold and scanned the entire showroom. He had the reputation of being able to home in quickly and precisely on the finest pieces of inventory. In junkyards and in shops filled with priceless antiques alike, that which was beautiful or the best example of its kind drew his infallible eye. Taylor "never forgot beautiful things. He constantly absorbed everything he saw and banked it, to be a source of reference." Taylor imparted this depth of sensitivity to his clients. He made them aware that "it's got to sing and talk back to you, and be A plus, plus if it crosses the threshold" of your house.

One of Taylor's first vignettes in the loft was a small bedroom that featured a French brass bed with porcelain finials and a pale-yellow Venetian cabinet. Taylor recalled in *California Living* that "Nini Martin came in and bought it, lock, stock, and barrel, for her oldest daughter." The bedroom also caught the attention of the editors at *House & Garden* magazine. They photographed it at the Martins' Hillsborough, California, home for the February 1957 cover of the magazine. This was Taylor's first cover with *House & Garden*, and the coveted endorsement of his work was a significant achievement. The magazine's fascination with him, and the Martin commission, continued in the next two issues. The magazine showcased the Martins' luxurious all-white living room, accented with cornflower blue and the mellow patina of

antique pine, on its March 1957 cover. The April 1957 issue ran an article entitled "Preview of Leisure Furniture" that featured the Martins' garden terrace. The *House & Garden* editors seriously considered featuring a third interior from the Martin home on the cover of that same April issue. However, they decided, reluctantly, that three consecutive covers of one interior designer's work, although it was "lively, fresh, and very different," would not be politic. The *House & Garden* attentiveness to the Martin commission foreshadowed a fruitful and long-standing relationship between Taylor and the magazine. *House & Garden* devoted a record eighteen covers and more than one hundred articles to his work over a period of thirty years. The editors of "Madison Avenue's slick magazines" were always asking, "What's new of Michael's work? His rooms, full of flowers and light, sold more copies for them than any designer in the world."

House & Garden again featured one of Taylor's sunny and white-washed rooms on its August 1960 cover. The shop vignette, his interpretation of a great room in a mill house in Provence, was accented with lush greenery and touches of milk- and deep blues. Glazed white quarry floor tiling and custom-fabricated pine beams painted white gave the vignette the Taylor quality. A cast-plaster coffee table and desk, two new signature pieces of Taylor's, also contributed to the textured or tactile dimension of this famous vignette. To ensure that it received the attention he thought it deserved, he staged it in the storefront window abutting Elizabeth Arden's courtyard.

And Arden's clientele responded. They flocked to Taylor's shop, where three key employees attempted to keep their fearless, challenging, and highly spirited employer grounded. Bill Johnson was Taylor's expeditor. He was a stocky no-nonsense man who navigated the me-

House & Garden magazine, March 1957.

House & Garden magazine, August 1960.

chanics of the business effectively for many years. Deirdre de Gay Fortman was a very proper British matron. She served as the punctilious gatekeeper and tended to the showroom customers. Geneva Hawkins, an early investor in Taylor's business, was his office manager and project estimator. A sweet and refined small woman, she fended off Taylor's creditors and juggled his chaotic finances to get the bills paid. Hawkins often used her own money to keep the business solvent. Taylor's unparalleled taste and talent were surpassed only by his undisciplined and self-indulgent extravagances. He bought whatever he wanted, whether he could afford it or not.

Taylor lived as grandly as he designed. In his frequent travels, he always stayed in palatial suites at the finest hotels. Every Christmas without exception he enjoyed a luxurious month-long sojourn at the Royal Hawaiian Hotel, staying in his favorite corner suite overlooking Waikiki Beach. He was accompanied until just after the New Year by his twice-widowed mother, Grace Paxton. Taylor's annual hotel bill, which also included one of his many Christmas presents to Paxton— treating her to the Hawaiian vacation—was at least seventy thousand dollars during the 1970s and the 1980s. At the Royal Hawaiian, Taylor claimed, he felt at home because Frances Elkins had decorated the hotel. He liked to walk through the lobby and make sure that people knew him.

Taylor's annual trips abroad might last two to three months at a time, and once he traveled for practically an entire year. On one occasion, while visiting Paris, he insisted that the staff at his hotel neatly pack and airmail his soiled laundry to Hawkins in San Francisco. She in turn sent it to Taylor's preferred laundry and dry cleaner in Chicago. There it was laundered or cleaned and then promptly returned to Tay-

lor in Paris. Although Taylor's liberal behavior and unmanageable spending habits exasperated Hawkins, she was devoted to him. Taylor had a big heart. He could be irresistible and endearing, even when he was frank and critical. However, even the normally devoted Hawkins could lose her patience with him. She once threw a telephone at him in a fit of anger.

Taylor could also become extremely agitated and irreverent. His quick wit, characteristic charm, and wicked, slightly naughty sense of humor could turn to biting rage when he did not get his way. He often exploded when a client did not buy into an idea of his or a vendor did not follow through with a commitment or an employee or contractor did not perform up to Taylor's own Herculean standards. The larger-than-life Taylor was not to be toyed with. He took his work, his opinions, and his responsibility to his clients very seriously. Creating and designing were Taylor's lifeblood. "He worked terribly, terribly hard. In the midst of a party, he'd sit down and work on sketches." Taylor's cardinal goal was to engage his clients, "to get them totally immersed and passionate about their collaboration with him." He wanted them to react and commit to what he was proposing for them. In the process, Taylor challenged many of his clients about their design choices, prompting him to realize that, in the end, "the worst bitches got the best houses!"

In San Francisco, Taylor met with clients either at their homes or occasionally in his private office, which was situated, along with Hawkins's office, in the shop's back quarters. He rarely appeared in the showroom. Taylor's office was very basic and oddly subdued given his prominence and titanic ego. The office, a field of "Michael Taylor White," was small, merely fourteen feet by sixteen feet, and dominated

"Syrie Maugham" bedroom, second rendition, 1957.

Opposite: Tour de Decours, San Francisco Museum of Art, 1960.

by a massive worktable lit by a bouillotte lamp. The table's glossy white milk-glass surface shimmered beneath voluminous piles of scattered papers, arrays of sketches, and fabric samples. Taylor spent long and arduous workdays, which frequently overlapped into the night, in this room. He sustained his energy and curbed his weight by drinking Metracal in large balloon-shaped stemware. Floor-to-ceiling cubbyholes, each stacked with neatly folded fabric samples arranged by color, lined two of the office walls. Taylor elevated himself during meetings. He always sat on a tall stool with his back toward the wall directly under ceiling spotlights, "illuminating him to handsome, intimidating advantage" while facing his clients, who sat at regular height in chairs.

When Taylor interviewed prospective clients, it could become "a relentless interrogation" and one that lasted several hours. Taylor did not take everyone. He turned down more than he accepted. Those he selected he chose for his sense that they would be willing to commit themselves to his will completely—although there were a few notable exceptions. Taylor prided himself on solving the design challenges that were specific to each client. His mission was to create interiors that were personal and appropriate to each individual's needs. He was, however, an insisting and exacting man, an artist who expected the same commitment from his clients. The relationships he forged were

intensely personal. When Taylor accepted a new client, he was also enriching his extended family. And he cherished that family greatly.

Taylor also built his regional and then national recognition through the designer showcases in which he participated early in his career. In the 1950s and the 1960s, these designer showcases were regularly held in civic or community buildings—not in private houses as they commonly are today. Taylor's first showcase occurred in 1957, when he was invited to design a room setup for one of San Francisco's first showcases. The other invitees constituted a group of some of the most prominent designers in the country, including the East Coast decorators Dorothy Draper (1889–1969) and William Pahlmann (1907–1987). The 1957 showcase was held at the Masonic Temple on Nob Hill for the benefit of the Lighthouse for the Blind.

Taylor created a setup that was reminiscent of the all-white bedroom that appeared in *Vogue*. He furnished the showcase bedroom with a pair of pickled-pine and painted Syrie Maugham Regency tester beds, dressing them in opaque Fortisan hangings, spreads, and skirts. Taylor also repeated the white-and-green Syrie Maugham fireside armchairs and the English chinoiserie benches, cushioning them the second time around in lettuce-green silk jacquard.

Taylor's first showcase, with its freshness and clarity of color, was a tremendous success. In fact, at the close of the event, he replicated the bedroom for a client, which *House & Garden* featured in their October 1957 issue.

Another showcase event that drew particular attention to Taylor's work was the 1960 Tour de Decours, an annual happening sponsored by the San Francisco Museum of Art under the auspices of the museum's women's board. Each member of the board invited an interior designer to create a model room that was then displayed in the museum. Taylor's sponsor was Dorothea Walker. Walker, a longtime contributing editor to *Vogue* and *House & Garden*, was an early enthusiast of Taylor's work. In her editorial assignments to search out talented interior designers in northern California, Walker discovered Taylor during the late 1940s and was responsible for introducing his work to *Vogue* and *House & Garden*.

Taylor's model room at the museum was an intimate dining vignette within a pavilion of whitewashed treillage. The effect was markedly reminiscent of the rooftop gazebo at Elizabeth Arden. The small round dining table and the four chairs were *equipales*, handcrafted Mexican furniture made of cedar strips and pigskin. Taylor had them sprayed glossy white at a local auto body shop. Taylor often specified this furniture for his clients. He purchased it, along with an infinite assortment of imported furniture and wares, at Cost Plus, the emporium-like store that was founded in 1958 on San Francisco's Fisherman's Wharf. Taylor liked contrast, and he was talented at blending humble and primitive pieces with rare and priceless antiques. The unconventional mixture elevated the ordinary pieces and also dressed down the formality of an interior, making it seem less precious.

The *equipales* were certainly fitting for the jewel-like pavilion, where the lush greens of tall palms intermingled with profuse arrangements of white Miltonia orchids. This contrasted strikingly with the overall mood of crispness and was reflected brilliantly in a shell-encrusted wall mirror, a pair of mirrored flower containers, and the silver and crystal tableware. On seeing the completed room, Walker remarked to Taylor that it reminded her of the Chambre d'Amour at Biarritz or the Costa Brava and joked that all it needed was a little sand. He took her off-the-cuff suggestion seriously and immediately

sent for three sacks of salt from the Leslie Salt Works Company. The trellised pavilion, with its imaginative and textural white "sand" floor, was now complete. The room was a success and perpetuated Taylor's name as a major American designer. *House & Garden* gave the arrangement a full page in the magazine.

Taylor's triumph with a white-on-white tableau also appealed to Elva Ryan, a long-standing and devoted friend of his who was one of his first clients in San Francisco. Elva and her husband Michael Ryan met Taylor through their daughter, Delores Ryan. She and Taylor had many friends in common. Taylor first visited the Ryans in 1949, when they were living in a spacious full-floor cooperative apartment in San Francisco. Although the Jackson Street apartment was already handsomely decorated, Taylor contributed a small touch to the home. He selected a carved Italian console table, a simple gilt mirror, and a pair of freestanding columns for its marble-floored entrance hall. A decade later, Taylor's professional relationship with the Ryans advanced significantly when he decorated a large house for them in Pacific Heights in an all-beige color scheme. The large living room, with a balanced pair of fireside banquettes upholstered in narrow-wale beige corduroy, a rare twelve-panel coromandel screen, and black Spanish carpets that floated on black wooden floors, was especially striking. Two years after Taylor completed this commission, Michael and Elva Ryan purchased an eleven-acre estate with a stable and a riding ring in Woodside, California, thirty miles south of San Francisco, on the Peninsula. The Ryans' new house, a rambling white adobe where initially they lived only during the summer months, was where Taylor specified his first white-on-white room for a client.

The Woodside commission triggered Frances Moffat's witty 1961 "Inside Society" column in the *San Francisco Examiner*: "Two Mikes in Her Life." Moffat, the legendary society columnist of the *Examiner*, wrote on the significant role that Taylor played in Ryan's life. "When Mrs. Michael Ryan says, 'Mike won't let me take this apartment,' or 'Mike doesn't like that color,' don't be fooled, she is not referring to her husband." The Mike to whom she was referring was Michael Taylor. He mentored "her in all things relating to décor."

Taylor called the Ryans' living room and adjacent sunroom and dining room "the great white plague." The walls and the ceilings in all three rooms were paneled completely in natural-colored knotty pine. Soon after the Ryans moved into their new house, Taylor sat in an armchair in the sunroom while staring up at its ceiling and twitching his hands in a by-then familiar gesture. "Do those knots make you nervous?" he asked them. Taylor's fervent critique compelled the Ryans to hire a painter. He was on a ladder for an entire year, painstakingly puttying the knots and painting the paneling white in all three rooms. Meanwhile the Ryan family went about their daily life in the house. Bill, the painter, practically became a member of the family.

The Ryans' young grandchildren were also treated to inspirational interiors in the Woodside house. Michelle Dana's bedroom had a four-poster bed with a delicate white canopy, a restful and restrained design that Taylor favored throughout his career. The bedroom belonging to Michelle's younger cousins, Dana and Michael Jackson, was outfitted with twin beds, red bedspreads, and a calfskin rug. Colorful and animated wall murals of clowns, painted by the boys' mother, Jeanne Ryan Jackson, who is herself a gifted artist and was a lifelong client and loyal friend to Taylor, enhanced the appropriately fun and youthful spirit of the room.

Taylor's superb taste and boundless attention to detail became as much a signature as his color palette and use of natural textures. One

Christmas season, the Dana family received a Cartier holiday card. It was in off-white, bordered in green, and exquisitely engraved with the motif of a gossamer pinecone perched atop a sprig of pine. When Michelle glanced at the face of the card, she turned to her mother, who was about to open it, and exclaimed, "Isn't that chic? It must be from Michael Taylor!" Delores called Taylor immediately to tell him the story. He roared with laughter over the telephone, serenaded by a chorus of laughter from his nearby staff, to whom he boastfully repeated the story while Delores was telling it to him. Michelle was right. Taylor had sent the card.

Maryon Davies Lewis, the daughter of Ralph K. and Louise Davies, was another early client who was a close and devoted friend of Taylor's. She, like her father before her, also backed Taylor financially. Lewis discovered Taylor when she wandered into his shop during the 1950s. Taylor first decorated for Lewis in 1955, beginning with an apartment in San Francisco. The one-bedroom apartment was small, but Taylor dramatized its interiors with a red, black, and white color scheme. In 1958, Lewis moved into a contemporary Gardner Dailey house on Jackson Street, which Taylor decorated in green and white. Lewis's next house, which she purchased in 1963, was a beige-colored Mediterranean-style villa perched on the pinnacle of Pacific Heights. The house overlooked San Francisco Bay, the Golden Gate Bridge, and Alcatraz. Lewis's stately house was perfect for Taylor's overscaled design, starting in the thirty-foot-long gallery that swept from the front door, past the main staircase and the dining room, before terminating at the entrance to the living room.

Lewis's living room was chronicled in the February 1968 *Time* magazine article "Decorators: The Mix Masters." The *Modern Living* feature proffered an overview of the decorating profession, deriving tremendous insight from nine of America's most accomplished interior decorators, including Taylor, Sister Parish (1910–1994), and Billy Baldwin (1903–1983), who referred to Taylor as "the golden boy" because he was an up-and-coming young star in decorating. The coverage was especially attentive to Taylor and Lewis's living room, which was captured in a handsomely composed color photograph taken by Fred Lyon, the preeminent photojournalist. Lyon's photograph was the lead for the eight-page article. In the photograph, which was the only full-page picture in the article, Lewis is pictured sitting on a love seat, gazing up at Taylor, who stands authoritatively to her right, facing her, while resting his right hand on a Louis XVI armchair that sits in his foreground. Taylor, dressed impeccably in a black suit for the photograph, had left nothing to chance in preparing for the photo session. With his usual candor, he telephoned Jim Ludwig, the vice president and regional manager of Saks Fifth Avenue in northern California at the time, and told him "to do something about Maryon's clothes."

Taylor was also astute and opinionated about fashion, which he believed was "very close to our work." He considered Coco Chanel to have influenced his own work. First and foremost in Taylor's eyes was Chanel's small apartment above her Paris salon on Rue Cambon. Taylor described the apartment as the most creative and exciting interior he had ever been in. He was stimulated by the overscaled furniture in the apartment's intimate interiors, and the mixture of unusual accoutrements, including large chandeliers by Robert Goosens—the accomplished costume-jewelry designer who created pieces for Chanel—Russian mirrors, and antique bronze deer.

Taylor could be extremely judgmental of his clients' attire. When visiting them at their home, he was renowned for telling them to change their clothes if he thought they didn't look good in the sur-

Michael Taylor and Maryon Davies Lewis in her Pacific Heights living room, *Time* magazine, February 1968.

roundings that he had created for them. Lewis, however, undeterred by Taylor's critique, selected her own outfit, a knee-length white silk shift that was patterned in an abstract pink-and-lime-green print, underscored perfectly by her pink shoes, which were also trimmed in a subtle band of lime green.

Taylor received further recognition in 1964, when he was included in an historical and beautiful book, *The Finest Rooms*, that profiled the so-called "Old Guard Decorators" currently practicing their trade in America.

The concept for the profile originated with Albert Hadley during the time that he was working at McMillen Inc., one of America's most prestigious interior design firms. The original idea was a serialized magazine feature. Unfortunately, his timing was off. The articles never came to fruition.

The idea resurfaced, however, soon after Hadley had started working with Sister Parish in 1962, when she asked him to join her in a meeting scheduled with Katharine Tweed, who was to interview her for a proposed book, *The Finest Rooms*. As it turned out, she was

Portrait of Michael Taylor by Wilbur Pippin.

on the same track as Hadley, and they took it from there when Hadley told Tweed of his original concept and that he had gone so far as to work with his good friend, the photographer Wilbur Pippin, to photograph what he called the "Old Guard," his friends and mentors, before approaching a favorite magazine with the idea. Hadley also told Tweed that he had included Michael Taylor, a young California decorator whose work was "new and fresh."

As work on the book progressed, Pippin generously allowed his eight photographs to be used—at Hadley's insistence—on the book's dust cover, since there was no plan to incorporate the decorators' images along with their essays in the book. In the end, Michael Taylor and his essay, "A New Look at Decorating," which emphasized that a room should be beautiful but not too perfect, "made up the final chapter in Tweed's extraordinary book, heralding him as the rising star of the younger generation."

Although Taylor decorated predominantly in California, he was sought after and hired by clients from all over the world. One such client was Jimmie Wilson, an heir to a prosperous second-generation tomato and melon farming and distribution business. Wilson's family agricultural operation, which was overseen by his sister, was based on their ranch in the Estacíon Bamoa, located in the state of Sinaloa, Mexico. The distribution division of the business, which Wilson ran, was handled in Nogales, Arizona where the family had maintained a summer house on "Banker's Row" since the 1940s.

Wilson admired Taylor's taste and asked a family friend, who was an early client of Taylor's, to introduce them. The Wilsons' simple beige stucco house in Nogales had experienced two electrical fires by the early 1960s, and Wilson wanted Taylor to renovate it. Although updating the family house had been the original intention of Wilson

and his widowed mother, Esther Wilson, it quickly became apparent that, once Taylor started altering the house, it would have been much easier and considerably less expensive to raze it and start anew. Taylor's initial vision for his projects always developed into infinitely grander circumstances as the job progressed. Taylor's vision was his only concern. "He had no regard for money as long as it wasn't his." If a client complained to Taylor about being "out of money," he would state, unequivocally, "Get more and call me when you have it!" Even if Taylor's clients didn't have the money, or chose not to do something he suggested, "He'd go ahead and do it anyways."

Taylor intended to create a monumental showplace for the Wilson family. He asked Charles Porter and Bob Steinwedell, the talented San Francisco architectural team with whom he often worked, to collaborate with him on the project. Wilson, as well, had cultivated taste and his own definite preferences for the new house. His favorite place was Capri, where he often rented a villa during the summer months and entertained his wide circle of friends, including Taylor. The house in Nogales, which sat on a one-and-one-half-acre hillside site overlooking downtown Nogales and the United States–Mexico border, would be inspired by the Mediterranean architecture of the celebrated island resort.

Taylor and Wilson embarked on a European sojourn together, while Porter and Steinwedell, who had visited the site in Nogales, began planning the house from their office in San Francisco. Taylor, with his voracious appetite for everything that was extraordinary and fitting, helped Wilson procure roomfuls of baronial antiques, rare tapestries, and even the façade of a building for the new house. One afternoon in Rome, Taylor and Wilson were strolling up the Spanish Steps. Taylor was intrigued with the façade of a building that he noticed out of the corner of his eye. Without warning, he guided Wilson into the building, which housed a silver shop, and gregariously introduced himself to the shop's owner. In short order, he had persuaded the owner to sell the façade. Taylor knew that its oversized wooden window casings and fanciful shutters, all aged with a weathered patina, would be unique and appropriate appointments for the Wilsons' house.

The European buying spree did not end with the façade. Through their good friend Eddie Holler, the knowledgeable and seasoned furniture and decorative arts dealer, Taylor and Wilson also found an early eighteenth-century Italian Baroque marble staircase with a balustrade of veined salmon marble. Holler discovered the staircase, disassembled, in a vast outdoor market of architectural details on the outskirts of Rome. Taylor was ecstatic about the staircase, which he had shipped to Nogales at great effort and expense. Taylor, as usual, expended whatever risk and effort was necessary for something that he "had to have." Often the outcome did not turn out as planned. In the instance of the staircase, its overscaled proportions rendered it too long for the Wilsons' entrance hall. Its sweep to the second floor of the house was also diametrically opposite to that of Porter and Steinwedell's irreversible floor plan. Taylor reacted to the situation with his typical nonchalance. He merely stored the staircase, along with a vast collection of other artifacts, in a dark and drafty warehouse in San Francisco, where it remained in pieces until his death nearly twenty years later.

Taylor's resourcefulness, however, was usually much more fruitful. When Taylor suggested to Esther Wilson that she give her son an assemblage of antique oak parquet for his birthday, the flooring, which Taylor had purchased in Versailles, France, was insufficient for its intended use—outfitting the house's library, coffee room, and six bedroom suites. In order to compensate for the shortage, Taylor fabricated additional parquet, which he then left outside in the variable Arizona climate for several months. The hot sun mixed with rain effectively weathered and aged the custom-made flooring, allowing him to intermingle it discreetly and successfully with the antique pieces.

Endless shipments of furniture, artwork, and accessories, all bought by Taylor and Wilson during their rapturous journey, poured into Nogales for the new house. The house became an imposing Mediterranean-style palazzo, fronted by a stone courtyard and bordered by a gated wall. It was truly a sanctuary. Its grand rooms, all of which opened on to an intermingling series of balustraded courtyards, terraces, and verandas, became familiar to scores of family members and friends. Family and holiday celebrations as well as customary social gatherings were regularly held there.

Taylor's work on his comprehensive plan for the Wilson compound spanned over a decade. Wilson, who was Taylor's greatest patron, gave Taylor free rein, indulging him in his illimitable creativity. Wilson was clearly aware of the extravagances, but "he had a very good time doing it" and "loved what [Taylor] did."

Taylor's fantastic rise led to a gilt-edged client roster. Among the more notable were John and Dodie Rosekrans. As with many of Taylor's most important clients, Mr. and Mrs. Rosekrans also became lifelong clients and devoted friends of the designer. The Rosekranses, who were newly married in 1960, moved at the time into John's family house on Washington Street in Pacific Heights. The renowned Beaux-Arts mansion, known as the Spreckels mansion, had been divided into four apartments for family members. Rosekrans and his wife lived in a two-bedroom apartment that occupied the first floor. Although the apartment had already been traditionally furnished and decorated by Alma Spreckels, Rosekrans's grandmother, the Rosekranses hired Taylor to do some work on their new home. Taylor concentrated on the master bedroom, which he furnished in his trademark overscaled white plaster furniture. Large-scale furniture enabled Taylor to simplify his interiors. He eschewed clutter, which prompted one of his favorite expressions: "When you take things out, you must increase the size of what's left."

Taylor's next assignment for the Rosekranses came in 1961 when they purchased a Tudor-style house, also in Pacific Heights, overlooking San Francisco Bay. The house included an oak-paneled library and an oblong dining room, which Taylor decorated in green and white. The library was done in earth tones. A cream-colored wool rug edged in very large tassels anchored it. Although Taylor loved the rug (he did not like wall-to-wall carpet), he decided to eliminate the tassels several years later. One day, while visiting Dodie Rosekrans, he walked into the library with her and said, "I think we should get rid of those tassels." Within seconds, both Taylor and Rosekrans were on their hands and knees. With scissors in hand, they cut off the tassels.

Taylor scored a particular coup in furnishing the Rosekranses' house when in 1967 he and Dodie Rosekrans attended the three-day Butterfield & Butterfield auction of the estate of Celia Tobin Clark. Clark, who was an heiress to the Hibernia banking fortune, had built one of the last great houses in the San Francisco region. The Cotswold-style manor house, named House-on-Hill, was located in Hillsborough, California, an affluent community south of San Francisco. The house was furnished with a collection of eighteenth-century French and English furniture, carpets, and rare objects that had been assembled in Europe during the 1920s by Clark and David Adler, her es-

teemed architect. (Adler was the older brother of Frances Elkins.) Taylor and Rosekrans knew the significance of Clark's home and its exceptional furnishings. With Taylor's encouragement, Rosekrans was a successful bidder at the auction many times over.

Diana Dollar Hickingbotham was another of Taylor's most important clients. Mrs. Hickingbotham first met Taylor when she attended a reception at his shop on Post Street. She was immediately enamored with him and his extraordinary taste. As she recalls, she decided on the spot that "if I ever do another house, I'll have him." Hickingbotham initially hired Taylor to do some work on the Hickingbothams' Victorian house in San Rafael, California. Unfortunately, her plans were halted because her husband, Joseph Hickingbotham, died. Taylor eventually decorated the first of four houses for Hickingbotham when, as a widow, she moved to San Francisco in 1967.

Hickingbotham purchased a classical brick and limestone townhouse on Jackson Street in Presidio Heights. Sandy Walker, the gifted San Francisco architect who was helped professionally by Taylor when Walker cofounded the architectural firm Walker and Moody, collaborated with Taylor on the renovation of the intimately scaled house. One of their most difficult tasks was altering the entire back of the house where a large bay window was to be added to the second-floor library. This decision was typical of Taylor's constant quest to expand the visual parameters of an interior by enhancing its sources of natural light.

When Taylor and Walker completed the townhouse, Hickingbotham thought of it as "a jewel box." *House & Garden* and *Architectural Digest* both agreed. However, much to Hickingbotham's chagrin, *House & Garden* chose to feature her housekeeper's attic sitting room on their March 1971 cover. The cheerful, sun-filled room was decorated in bright yellow, pink, and green. It also was accessorized with a bank of pink hydrangeas. These were one of Taylor's favorite flowering plants, which he comically referred to as "hydraneas." Equally flattering to Hickingbotham's house was *Architectural Digest's* 1973 article, titled "San Francisco Classic." The article, which highlighted the principal rooms, was the first in what would become the magazine's long-term coverage of Taylor.

Although Taylor's work was primarily residential, restaurateurs and hoteliers also sought his expertise. During the early 1960s, Victor Bergeron, the celebrated proprietor of Trader Vic's, hired Taylor to spiff up the restrooms at his San Francisco restaurant. Taylor specified authentic zebra skin–wrapped doors for both restrooms and walls of authentic zebra skin in the men's division. The ladies' division was decorated in lava rock and mirrored walls. Trader Vic's, one of San Francisco society's favorite watering holes, came to be known as having "the most gorgeous restrooms in San Francisco."

Claude Rouas, an aspiring San Francisco restaurateur, commissioned Taylor to decorate his first restaurant, L'Etoile, during the late 1960s. L'Etoile was located in the Huntington Hotel on Nob Hill. It was the successor to three restaurants that had already failed at the same location. Nob Hill was unpopular at the time, and Dolly Fritz, the owner of the hotel, wanted to attract hotel and dinner guests and also to offer room service. Taylor, who had always wanted to get his hands on the restaurant, assured Rouas, his wife Ardath, and Rouas's business partner Henri Barberis that he could create an "in place," even though they gave him a limited budget—which he adhered to— and only three weeks to complete the work.

Taylor delivered as promised. He reworked the interior of the previous restaurant, first by thinking out the entire process of how the space should flow. Taylor mirrored behind the bar and also installed four sets of full-length draped mirrors around the perimeter of the room. He believed "that people loved to look at themselves." For further effect, he mounted a zebra head above the bar and put an elephant foot in one corner of the room to be used as a planter. The overall game-hunting decor was also enhanced by leopard-printed velour tablecloths and wall-sconce lampshades that Ardath's mother made for the restaurant.

In the dining room, Taylor retained the existing seating, due to the budgetary constraints of his clients. Booths upholstered in pink Naugahyde outlined the perimeter of the rectangular-shaped room. Two rows of booths were placed back-to-back in the center of the room. The conjoining of the booths created a generous platform where Taylor placed a pair of large stone Grecian urns, which were always filled with huge arrangements of fresh flowers. The effect of the decor in the dining room was to make its guests feel attractive. There was a restful and pleasant glow that radiated from the soft gray walls, whose paneled divisions were trimmed in dark gray and inset with mirrors. A large crystal chandelier, hung in the center of the dining room, sparkled along with an outlining sequence of fringed metal wall sconces.

Before L'Etoile's opening night, Taylor sat in every booth to ensure that the lighting was good and that nothing would glare in a customer's face. He also designed the pink-and-burgundy menu, insisting that it should not be large and obtrusive. Taylor wanted L'Etoile's patrons to see their surroundings and be engaged by everything that was happening. When he completed his decoration, he told Rouas, "I've done all I can do." He then added, "I hope the food is good." He also

House & Garden magazine, March 1971.

offered to take back all of his decoration if the restaurant didn't succeed. Fortunately, L'Etoile opened with a bang and experienced a lengthy and successful run.

In 1970, Rouas and Barberis again turned to Taylor for his invaluable guidance. L'Etoile's success had motivated the restaurateurs to take over the ownership of Fleur de Lys, located in Union Square. Initially, Rouas, his brother Maurice Rouas, and Barberis planned to create a simple French country bistro, but San Francisco's taste level "didn't want simple." Fleur de Lys's clientele demanded good wines and superb food. Taylor was emphatically unimpressed with the restaurant when he saw it for the first time. He asked his clients, "Have you already signed the lease? I can't do anything with this dump!" The lease had already been signed, so Taylor got to work right away.

Taylor transformed the restaurant by tenting the interior in its entirety. Originally, he planned to order seven hundred and fifty yards of fabric needed for the tenting from Spain, but because the fabric factory was shut down for their annual August vacation, the order would have taken five to six months to fill. His clients could not wait. Taylor improvised in his usual fashion, following the advice of Russell Mac-Masters. MacMasters was a good friend who became a prominent lighting specialist as well as the photojournalist who documented the majority of Taylor's work that appeared in *Architectural Digest*. Mac-Masters knew a lot of students at the San Francisco Art Institute. His idea was to hire a barrage of them to hand-screen the authentic weighty sailcloth that he procured from a ship's chandlery in Oakland, California.

The colossal project was undertaken in a chicken factory on lower Broadway in San Francisco. Cedric Smith, the artist, acted as the foreman. He oversaw the dozens of incredibly talented student artists, who worked in shifts around the clock for three weeks, screening the fabric while wearing gas masks. The screening was done with eight different stencils, custom cut by silk-screen experts. The four-foot-wide stencils, which ranged from eight feet to twelve feet in height, were placed one at a time over the sailcloth that lay on a custom-made platform. The eight colors of textile paint formulating the sixteenth-century Indian pattern were spread uniformly across the screens with a squeegee. Once the screening was complete, the fabric was sent to Los Angeles for flameproofing.

Taylor hired one of his upholsterers to install the sailcloth in the restaurant. He ingeniously suspended the brightly colored fabric from a large wooden donut that was mounted to the center of the dining room ceiling. The gathered fabric billowed down in luxurious proportions to the cornice line, where it melded into full-length curtains that draped the entire room. The curtains were tied back at intervals, which allowed access into the private dining room, the bar, and the kitchen and also exposed several large mirrored panels that Taylor installed to amplify the interior, implying that there were passageways leading into additional tents.

Fleur de Lys, like L'Etoile, quickly became a favorite of San Francisco's stylish crowd. Rouas, who now had two successful restaurants to his name, hailed Taylor as an "important tool" to his success. The magical partnership between the two men would prove to scale even greater heights in the years to come.

The year 1969 was pivotal in both Taylor's personal and his professional life. For many years, he had been living in a small Gardner Dailey flat on Telegraph Hill. However, he was increasingly enticed by San Francisco's Sea Cliff neighborhood. He had received several calls about a 1930s beige stucco Mediterranean-style house from real estate brokers, and one day he drove out to see it. Lita Vietor, his long-time friend and client, accompanied him. When Taylor and Vietor arrived at the house, they "opened the gate, walked through the garden, opened the front door and looked right through into the Pacific Ocean, crashing onto the rocks below." Taylor found himself immediately spellbound by the house and its spectacular site, which overlooked Baker Beach. He made an offer on the house, even though it was well out of his price range. The offer was accepted. Taylor's clients "pitched right in and paid their bills," enabling him to consummate the purchase.

Taylor set about making major changes to the first and second floors of the house, which included moving walls and installing fireplaces. He also gutted the lower-level storeroom to make space for his new office and studio, opening it up to the ocean with a wall of glass on its north side.

The lower level of the house was decorated in Taylor's "California Look." The floors were paved in Yosemite slate (Taylor coined the name to prevent his competition from locating the source). The walls were painted "Michael Taylor White." The focal point of the office, aside from the dramatic view, was Taylor's desk, a French Baroque sycamore game table on diamond-shaped stone pedestals. Taylor bought the table at an antiques shop in Paris. It was called a game table because it was used to butcher game birds at a grand chateau in the south of France. Taylor held court at the desk, sitting in a stag chair that he purchased at a San Francisco junk shop for sixty-five dollars. The chair, which was aptly scaled to Taylor's large physique, complemented the collection of eclectic objects that accessorized his work space, including a large Syrian mosaic of a strident lion, dried saguaro cacti, and Mexican geodes. Taylor was always rotating furniture and accessories in and out of the office-studio, staging it for both himself and his design staff of nine as they considered pieces for their steady succession of jobs.

Taylor's design for the first and second floors of his house was the antithesis of the lower level. Taylor, who preached to his clients "when in doubt, throw it out," did not follow his own advice when furnishing the Sea Cliff house. He did not "design the interior in any formal sense." He "just moved everything in." When Paige Rense, the editor of *Architectural Digest*, asked Taylor if she could photograph his house for the magazine, he told her, "You don't really want to photograph it, do you?" Taylor's house was the cover feature of the magazine's December 1977 issue.

Taylor's house was an "apocalypse." It was like "walking through the looking glass." He created an exotic visual fantasy, merging all the furniture and the collections that he loved. The jam-packed interiors, with their sixteen-foot-tall ceilings, were "more surreal than, over and beyond anything you'd anticipate finding in any of his clients' homes. It was him."

In the entrance hall, Taylor placed a mid-eighteenth-century Rococo painted console. Above it he hung a Yi Dynasty painting of a deer on silk. Although both of these pieces were precious, Taylor dressed down the vignette, using burlap upholstery on the walls as a backdrop. He also arranged on the terra-cotta-tiled hall floor, in front of a wall of glass, a grouping of antiquities. Stone geodes, marble and onyx busts of Roman emperors, and cast-stone capitals intermingled with an array of exotic plants, all beneath a Roman carved marble torso of Dionysius, the Greek God of wine and celebration. The statue stood on a pedestal, views of the Pacific Ocean and the Marin headlands beyond.

Fleur de Lys.

The entrance hall also served as a gallery that led to the dining room and the living room. The doorway into the dining room stepped up from the northwest corner of the entrance hall, by the wall of glass that overlooked the ocean. In the dining room, Taylor painted the preexisting redwood-paneled walls in reddish terra cotta and paved the floor in Yosemite slate. He outfitted the room with a diverse selection of pieces, including an Italian inlaid-marble pedestal table, a suite of black leather–upholstered Louis XIII provincial side chairs, and an Italian carved olivewood credenza. The accessories were also distinctive. There were pairs of Venetian Baroque polychromed gesso and carved statuettes, oversized blue-and-white jardinières, and Italian Baroque parcel-gilt columns. Moroccan-inspired grilles screened the wall of glass. Taylor purchased the wooden grille work from the estate of Adrian, the legendary Hollywood artist, costume designer, and American couturier whose salon was in Beverly Hills. He used them as the model for the door screens in the Wilson pool pavilion.

The living room was located across from the dining room, at the opposite end of the entrance hall. In the living room, natural light filtered through the longest expanse of glass in the house. Natural-colored bamboo blinds with an abbreviated drop tempered the glare

Left and above, top: Bedroom setup in Michael Taylor's office at Sea Cliff with wicker seating, woven and split-cane peacock armchairs and alder tree-trunk four-poster bed, and cedar stump and marble bedside tables; *middle*: "Jennifer" wicker seating, a wooden deer, and dried saguaro cacti poles; *bottom right*: game table desk, "Jennifer" wicker seating, stone geodes, and dried saguaro cacti poles.

from the ocean and infused an organic dimension into the room. The focal point of the living room was an early eighteenth-century French Régence carved liver-and-gray marble fireplace mantel that was never permanently affixed to the wall. (Taylor tried it out for seventeen years.) Taylor grouped the principal sofa and a pair of ivory linen velour–upholstered love seats around the mantel, along with an eclectic mixture of furnishings. These included an eighteenth-century six-panel black lacquer and gilt screen, a French Régence mirror in a carved gilt wood frame, and an Art Deco coffee table of black granite and ebonized wood. The sofa, which was upholstered in vibrant floral printed cotton canvas, came from Denning and Fourcade, the renowned New York interior design firm. Taylor purchased it at auction. Two late seventeenth-century Flemish tapestries lined the terra-cotta painted plastered walls and created a stirring backdrop for

additional compilations of furniture. There was a Louis XV *bureau plat*, a carved fruitwood library table, and a suite of rare Venetian Rococo carved gilt wood armchairs, all tempered by Taylor's requisite and densely scattered arrangements of plants, flowers, and soaring trees.

Taylor's second-floor master bedroom, which overlooked the ocean and the Golden Gate Bridge, was mystical. Yosemite slate served as the foundation for yet another barrage of wide-ranging antiques and accessories, all of which glowed against the terra-cotta patina of the plastered walls. Paramount to this arrangement was Taylor's elaborate Spanish Baroque carved gilt four-poster bed. It dictated the scale and magnitude of the pieces that were arranged throughout the plant-laden room. This included a pair of Italian Neoclassical carved gilt side chairs, Etruscan and pre-Columbian artifacts, and a George III gilt bocage table that was detailed organically with carvings of twigs,

Entrance hall at Sea Cliff.

Entrance hall at Sea Cliff. View is toward the Pacific Ocean and the Marin headlands.

vines, and reeds. Taylor also kept his favorite possession—a Sung Dynasty bronze deer that he purchased when he was nineteen (and paid off in ten years)—in the room.

Taylor's bedroom was the control center for his life and his business. His mornings always began with breakfast in bed, which was served to him by Hoy, his Chinese houseman. Taylor spent his mornings in his curtained bed, dressed in a Japanese silk robe, sketching or talking on one of his three bedside telephones. He gossiped the morning away with his clients and good friends, which included Maryon Davies Lewis, Dodie Rosekrans, Diana Knowles, Dede Wilsey, Frances Bowes, and Dorothy Fay, Bowes's mother. He also called downstairs to the studio to monitor the progress of his quaking staff and Bob Burdine. Burdine was the affable and proficient office manager who had succeeded Bill Johnson. His job was to keep peace in the office—where there was always a high turnover in personnel, even though Taylor mentored his employees consummately—and out in the field. Sometimes Taylor summoned Burdine or one of the staff to his bed-

room in order to discuss a pending issue or to test them, making sure they were on their toes. By one o'clock in the afternoon, Taylor emerged from his chamber, immaculately groomed, stylishly dressed, and ready to start the next phase of his day. He was usually running far behind schedule. Taylor's clients, associates, and friends were accustomed to waiting for him.

Several years after Taylor moved into the Sea Cliff house, he replaced the walled garden that fronted the house with a heated swimming pool. Although swimming pools were not in vogue in San Francisco due to the cold climate, Taylor, undeterred by convention, proceeded with his plans. Taylor's pool area was an oasis. To create the atmosphere, he had twenty-five-foot-tall cypress trees trucked in. The pool itself was set into a terrace of Yosemite slate. High beige sandstone coping followed the shapely outline of the pool. Taylor kept the water temperature very hot, which caused diaphanous clouds of steamy fog. A low sandstone wall and a lion's-head fountain stood at the east end of the pool. Meticulously placed potted plants, cast-stone

Multiple views of dining room at Sea Cliff.

Two views of the living room at Sea Cliff.

capitals, and massive ribbed globular terra-cotta pithoi, along with other unique objects, surrounded the pool and guided the way from the front gate to the main entrance of the house.

Although Taylor was content with his move from Sutter Street to Sea Cliff, he still yearned for a retail venue for his business. In 1972, following the recommendation of a friend, Taylor consigned pieces of his inventory to the Greenery on North Point Street in San Francisco. Bob Bell, the florist extraordinaire and a friend of Taylor's, created a basketball court–sized showroom by remodeling an auto repair shop for his horticultural design business. Bell did not need the vast front room of the warehouse, which well accommodated Taylor's signature overscaled pieces, including chair frames, doors, concrete furniture, and cement paintings by Laddie John Dill. Taylor's involvement in the venture lasted five years and was backed by Davies Lewis, but it was not particularly successful. In the end, the Greenery served more as a storage facility for Taylor than as a retail establishment.

Taylor also tried his hand at retailing in West Hollywood, California. In 1975, with the encouragement and liberal backing of Jimmie Wilson, Taylor opened a shop called Taylor, Wilson and House Ltd. on Melrose Place in West Hollywood. To acquire inventory, Taylor, Wilson, and Terry House, a friend of Wilson's, traveled extensively for

Two views of the living room at Sea Cliff, looking toward
the Pacific Ocean, the Marin headlands and the Golden
Gate Bridge.

Three views of the living room at Sea Cliff. *Clockwise:* View toward fireplace; close-up of fireplace; view toward Flemish tapestry, Louis XV commode, and eighteenth-century Venetian, Rococo, carved giltwood armchair.

Three views of the master bedroom. *Clockwise:* View toward carved and gessoed Louis XV chair, rustic table and Italian neoclassical painted commode and carved glitwood side chair; Spanish Baroque carved gilt four-poster bed and George III bocage table; view toward Golden Gate Bridge.

Left: Swimming pool at Sea Cliff.

Above: Michael Taylor standing by swimming pool, 1982.

three months throughout Brazil, Peru, Egypt, France, and South Africa. They gathered innumerable pieces for the new shop. In South America, they bought minerals and rock crystals as tall as six feet and weighing up to a ton. Taylor often introduced these organic objects as "sculpture in rooms and gardens." Taylor's custom-made cactus tree bed was distinctive to the inventory of antique and contemporary furniture. The bed poles, located by Taylor in Mexico, were made from "a very rare cactus that only grows in two places in the world." The shop also carried marquetry and bamboo furniture and fabrics that Taylor designed and had made in India.

Taylor, Wilson and House Ltd. was short-lived. The retail space was physically limiting, and Taylor's continuous traveling and exorbitant spending for the shop made it difficult to recoup the investment. Wilson's untimely death from a massive heart attack in 1977 also caused a major setback to Taylor, both financially and personally. Wilson was a gracious and generous human being. He was one of Taylor's closest friends.

Taylor, Wilson & House Ltd. store front.

Although Taylor was unsuccessful with his Melrose Place shop, he had a strong following in the Los Angeles area, dating back to 1953, when he was commissioned to decorate a house in Santa Monica. Thirteen years later, Stanley and Lynn Beyer hired Taylor to decorate their English-style whitewashed brick house in Bel Air. Taylor's initial collaboration with the Beyers was the first of six homes that he did for them. He also decorated two offices for Stanley. During the early 1970s, the Beyers decided to build a beach house on Point Lechuza in Malibu. When they showed their property to Taylor, he told them, "You can only have one architect, John Lautner." Lautner was an influential contemporary Los Angeles architect who had apprenticed with Frank Lloyd Wright. Taylor had already collaborated with Lautner on the Beverly Hills house of Gary and Liz Familian. The two designers shared the same philosophy concerning organic design.

Taylor, Lautner, and the Beyers envisioned a building that harmonized with the unparalleled beauty of the site. The house, which was fabricated completely in rough concrete, adhered to Lautner's objective. He "wanted to suit in every way this rocky point and create a durable, sheltered, livable outlook to the panorama of rocks, coves, beach, and ocean." The end result was a "large free-flowing space with a high sloping ceiling and window walls, a kind of observation deck" that looked as if it had grown naturally from the landscape.

Planning and building the Beyer house was no easy feat. Because of the restrictions of the Coastal Commission and various environmental originations, the house took ten years to complete. As it evolved through various stages of planning, five different designs for the house had to be submitted to the commission before it gave its final approval and issued a building permit. Taylor contributed to the challenges of building as well. He specified that most of the furniture

was to be incorporated into the architecture, creating a coherence in design between his work and Lautner's.

In planning the house, Taylor insisted that the site and the interior be punctuated with boulders. He felt that their presence would further integrate the house and its interiors with the natural setting. The task of locating the boulders fell to Richard Turner, the project's supervising architect. Turner, a resourceful person, obtained permission from a national organization to traverse their property that abutted the Three Rivers near Sequoia National Park in central California. The river was packed with boulders. Together, Turner and Stanley Beyer scoured the river. Over a period of six months, they accumulated a collection of 125 granite boulders, weighing from three to twenty-one tons each. New roads were bulldozed to the riverbed just for this project, which enabled hydro-cranes with seventy-foot boons to retrieve the enormous rocks.

Transporting the boulders required forty-foot-long flatbed trucks and nylon strapping, which coddled the rocks and prevented them from being scratched during the seven-hour trip to Malibu. Because each truck accommodated only two to three boulders apiece, it took several months to move them. The entire process was intricate, complicated, and very expensive. When the boulders reached Malibu, they were assembled on four acres of land near the Beyers' site. Taylor and Turner, assisted by a crew of six to eight men, inspected the boulders. Each rock was turned several ways in order to determine its most unusual profile. The rocks were also steam-cleaned and sealed to prevent fungal growth. Before the framing began, the twenty most unique of the lot were set in location on the sand, on concrete, or on concrete blocks within the footprint of the house. It would have been too difficult to position them inside the house after it was built. The rocks with flat surfaces became end tables. A few anchored some of the eighteen-foot-tall and one-half-inch-thick laminated glass windows. The remainder accentuated the interior. Additional boulders were scattered on the oceanfront terrace, throughout the property, and at the sea wall, where they blended naturally into the landscape.

The installation of the main floor was also a major task. Thick pieces of Yosemite slate measuring six feet by eight feet were trucked in from a quarry in northern California. On site, the stone pieces were laid out on the beach where, under the direction of Taylor and Turner, they were sawed and prearranged into free-form islands of slate. Once the islands were set on a structural slab inside the house, they were edged with mortar. Areas between were filled with concrete. The entire floor was then coated with a high-gloss sealer. Taylor ranked the Beyer house "among the best he's ever done." He found the experience exhilarating. He also admired his clients, "whose acumen was matched only by their stamina and taste."

Taylor's commission for Stanley and Lynn Beyer coincided with the project he undertook for Douglas S. Cramer, the legendary television producer who wanted to build a simple country house. Cramer considered locations for the house spanning from northern California's wine country all the way down the California coast to San Diego. He "wanted a place that was visually exciting," and "where the climate was good." Cramer found the ideal situation in the Santa Ynez Valley—thirty-five miles north of Santa Barbara.

Cramer purchased four hundred acres in the valley, amassing the verdant property for the ranch he christened La Quinta Norte. Cramer immediately began planning for the house he envisioned as three connecting pavilions with tall walls to showcase his comprehensive collection of contemporary art. He hired Peter Choate—the respected

Los Angeles architect—to design the buildings and Craig Johnson (Cramer's partner at the time) to design the landscape.

Cramer's next step was finding an interior decorator for the project. He chose Taylor, whose standing as "the preeminent California designer" and mastery of interiors that were organic and indigenous appealed to him. Cramer asked Denise Hale, the San Francisco socialite who was his long-standing friend and also a friend of Taylor's, to introduce the two men.

Hale, who thought Taylor "was very special, and had the magic touch," brokered the first meeting between Cramer and Taylor, which occurred over a lengthy two-hour lunch at Taylor's house in San Francisco. Although the two men gossiped during the first hour of the meal, the conversation ultimately developed into an intense interview during which Taylor interrogated Cramer about the prospective commission. He also reviewed Choate's architectural drawings, which Cramer brought to the meeting. Although Taylor "loved the project" and Cramer hoped he would give the blueprints the equivalent of a "papal blessing," Taylor had his own ideas for the house.

Several days after the meeting, Taylor visited Cramer and Johnson at the ranch where the charismatic setting and the bucolic landscape inspired him to rethink the house completely. Taylor asserted himself immediately. He "confronted the entire building process, leading Choate and Cramer into his concept of one large two story house." Within four months of the first meeting, the three pavilions on the property's terraced hillside, totaling ten thousand square feet, became "one towering armada," a main house with twenty-five thousand square feet. Taylor also relocated the ranch's guest house down the hill from the main house.

Other major changes ensued throughout the project. After the foundation for the main house was dug where Choate had sited it, "Taylor waved his magic wand," insisting the foundation "be moved three feet backwards from the road for a better view." Cramer accepted Taylor's sound and compelling advice, respecting him and recognizing that he was like "a force of nature you can't tackle." The decision was in concert with the "insane perfectionism" that governed the entire project: "Nothing took too much time, no quest for the right object would be cut short—whatever it took, the house had to be exactly as they [Cramer and Taylor] dreamed it."

When Taylor completed the interiors at the ranch, "he was so ingrained with the look and feel of the house" that he asked Cramer to not install the artwork for three days. He wanted him "to live with and enjoy *his* art." Cramer was finally "allowed" to hang the art after two days. All was well until Taylor arrived unexpectedly at the ranch to assess the installation. He "had a fit" over the Ellsworth Kelly painting hanging in the living room. The large blue-and-white canvas was oriented vertically, and Taylor wanted Cramer to turn it sideways—"to show off the room better." Cramer refused the request, only to be rebutted by Taylor's quick retort: "And why not? Kelly will never know the difference!"

By the late 1970s and the early 1980s, Taylor's renown was spreading internationally. The *Bangkok Post* proclaimed him as "interior designer extraordinaire" in their front-page feature about him. The *Bangkok World* followed suit when Taylor toured Thailand for a two-week antique shopping trip. He also received kudos in *Schoner Wohnen*, the German lifestyle magazine. The article about Taylor focused on his Sea Cliff house, which was lavishly illustrated in the twelve-page spread.

Taylor continued receiving challenging commissions. Among them was a project to decorate a newly built villa for a sheikh in Saudi

Interior, Taylor, Wilson & House Ltd.

Arabia. San Francisco architect Coby Everdell designed the project following traditional Islamic principles. Everdell, who was responsible for interviewing and finding the decorator for the job, recommended Taylor "because his style was perfect for a young couple in a warm climate."

The villa was built with two separate living rooms, located on opposite sides of a trapezoidal-shaped entrance hall. The living room to the right side of the hall was used for business entertaining. Women were not permitted there. Opposite was the family living room. One large staff kitchen, with separate pantries, situated at the back of the building served both living rooms.

Each living room was decorated distinctively. The business living room (the *majlis*) was furnished with a suite of "Jennifer" furniture. Taylor had recruited and hired Dennis Buchner, a design apprentice in Los Angeles for several years, to inventory and catalog everything in Taylor's house and warehouse. Under the title of executive vice president, Buchner selected twenty-five pieces from Taylor's existing collection that he reproduced, advertised, and distributed nationally under the designation "Michael Taylor Designs." The cornerstone of the collection was the lightweight fauxstone model of the "Jennifer" chair initially created for the actress Jennifer Jones Simon. When Taylor decorated Norton and Jennifer Jones Simon's Malibu compound during the 1970s, Jones "asked for a chair that was 'free and pillowy' but would not compete with the Simons' vast art collection." Taylor provided a wicker design with canvas-covered cushions. It was "big enough to lie down on or curl up in." Taylor judged the "Jennifer" furniture perfect for the Saudi Arabian desert. With the wicker pieces, he infused vibrant color into the business living room. He dotted the white-canvas cushioned sofas and chairs with his signature ball pillows in solid lime-green silk linen.

"Jennifer" chair, faux stone model.

"Jennifer" chair, wicker model.

The white Roman travertine floor, putty-colored leather area rug, and assortment of large stone tables introduced the "California Look" to Saudi Arabia.

The business living room, which contained a large sunken grotto for watching television, could also be converted into a discotheque. The disco lights were hidden in the center of the ceiling, and the sound equipment was concealed behind a large mirrored wall at one end of the room. When the wall was lit from behind, the mirrored effect disappeared, facilitating the room's use as a disco.

The family living room was furnished with an overstuffed sofa and several paired groupings of plump armchairs that were upholstered in glazed navy-blue floral chintz. Likenesses of magenta peonies and sinuous foliage dominated the printed fabric, the striking design of which also included medium-blue and lilac-shaded flowers. Solid magenta silk linen on the chair and banquette cushions sustained the engaging accent color. The travertine floor, leather area rug, and stone tables were in keeping with the business living room.

The family living room also contained a small kitchen, which opened on to the dining area. The dining table was large; a four-inch-thick rectangular rubbed-ash top sat on diamond-shaped concrete pedestals. Taylor angled the sides of the table top forty-five degrees at each end, increasing the number of guests that it could seat from eight to twelve. The oversized wicker dining chairs, with magenta seat cushions, added an organic element to the setting.

The two-story white plastered contemporary building was built around a large indoor swimming pool. Most of the rooms overlooked the atrium through windowed walls that were shuttered in sliding panels of teak trellis (*mashrabiyya*), which "veiled women from the gaze of men." The plant-filled atrium, with its travertine floor and roof of glass skylights, was light and airy. It was the epicenter of the walled villa, a self-contained world necessitated by the region's intensely hot climate.

Taylor decorated the atrium in a sea of color. A profusion of silk linen ball pillows, in solid shades of vibrant pink, orange, green, and blue, accented a pair of white canvas upholstered banquettes recessed into mirrored niches. A pair of solid rectangular travertine coffee tables fronted each banquette. A round travertine table with white rush-seated chairs sat between each banquette and the poolside bar.

A second sitting area balanced the bar on the opposite side of the pool. Here, Taylor specified a faux-stone sofa and a pair of chairs that Buchner adapted from the "Jennifer" model. They were also cushioned in white canvas. A travertine "waterfall" (three-sided) coffee table, accessorized with a pair of Taylor's signature heavy hockey-puck ashtrays, anchored the vignette.

The Saudi Arabian commission required Taylor to provide all the housewares for the villa. Kitchen equipment (specified by the clients' French chef), linens, and every accessory imaginable were purchased for the client. Suzanne Tucker, Taylor's design assistant since 1981 and heir apparent, oversaw that exhaustive task. She even

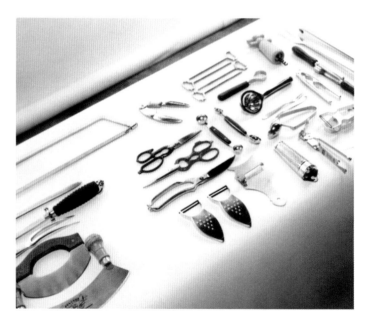

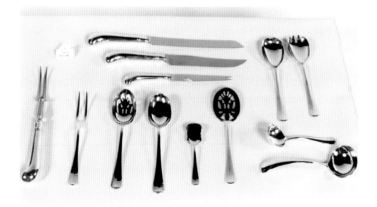

Housewares for Saudi Arabian commission.

selected the stainless and sterling-silver flatware, which was specified in the same pattern.

Every room was initially set up at Elwell Trucking and Storage in San Francisco, where Taylor inspected it. Then a professional photographer shot each vignette against a background of white seamless photography paper for the client's long-distance review and final approval prior to shipment. When all the material was assembled and shipped, Taylor made his way to Saudi Arabia. Although the sheikh and his wife had visited Taylor at his office in San Francisco, this was Taylor's first visit to the job site. He arrived in grand style, bringing along fifteen pieces of Louis Vuitton luggage. He was accompanied by Bob (Chuck) Husted, his significant other. Keith McLelland, Taylor's principal assistant on the job, had been sent on one week ahead of him to organize the installation. Everdell, the architect, arrived the day before Taylor. Together, the four men unloaded the two dozen crates that had been in transit from San Francisco for a month. They started at one end of the villa, working their way through the vast building until every room was furnished and accessorized according to plan. It took them two full weeks to complete the job despite the fact that Taylor sparred tyrannically with the sheikh's representative, who was overseeing the installation for his boss. Taylor did not take orders from his clients' employees—or from anyone else for that matter. He created a great scene over the unendurable arrangement and threatened to leave the job immediately—with his associates in tow. Fortunately, Everdell and McLelland conciliated Taylor, buffering all communications between the representative and him.

McLelland was of special interest to the local contractors who were still on site, finishing their work. His drill was a revelation to them. They had never seen a portable power drill. McLelland ended up selling the drill, attachments, accessories, and tool belt to the construction foreman on his final day at the site.

When the project was completed, Taylor and Everdell were honored at an informal celebratory dinner in the dining room. The sheikh, Taylor, Everdell, and Husted sat at the dining table. Together, they rejoiced in the accomplishment of creating this magnificent home. Taylor was especially moved and proud when, during the dinner, the sheikh removed his burgundy and intricately gold-embroidered caftan and placed it on Taylor's shoulders, proclaiming, "You are my brother!"

Taylor was also commissioned to help plan and decorate the Auberge du Soleil in the Napa Valley. The Auberge du Soleil was the long-standing vision of Claude and Ardath Rouas. In 1974, they purchased thirty-three acres of olive groves in the foothills of the Napa Valley. The Rouases visualized a restaurant whose culinary élan and rustic but sophisticated style would harmonize with the unspoiled verdant countryside. They wanted "their guests to feel like they were south of somewhere—not a specific place, but a feeling reminiscent of a romantic place in the sun where they might have traveled to, yet completely at home where it was."

In the spring of 1980, the Rouases proceeded with their plans. They invited Taylor and the architect Sandy Walker for a picnic lunch. Together, the Rouases, Taylor, and Walker sat "on a big rock, shaded by a circle of olive trees," overlooking the property while the Rouases imparted their vision to them. The Rouases knew that Taylor and Walker were the right choice for this venture. They were an excellent team.

A few days after the lunch, Walker presented his drawings to the Rouases. Walker was inspired by Sam Chamberlain's "wonderful book of drawings of different kinds of French country architecture" that he brought to the meeting and reviewed with Ardath. The proposed

Two set-ups for the Saudi Arabian commission at Elwells. *Top:* Dining room. *Bottom:* Wicker seating.

structure resembled a building that belonged to a French farm complex. He anchored the western end of the building with a tall conical-shaped feature that looked like a silo. The silo housed the bar. The design for the principal and remaining sections of the building implied that an outbuilding of the complex had been added to the silo. This contained the entrance lobby and restaurant. A windowed wall spanning the entire length of the southern elevation framed the best panorama of the Napa Valley.

Taylor also contributed to the design. He added an entry court, which accentuated the intimacy of Walker's plan. Taylor also suggested that an olive tree be planted in each corner of the walled courtyard. Under the direction of Jack Chandler, the project's landscape architect, fully grown trees were transported from the bottom of the hill by large cranes and painstakingly hoisted over the walls. Once the trees were placed, "everyone agreed that it changed the whole ambience of the entrance."

Selecting the building's exterior color was another challenge. Taylor and Ardath spent more than two weeks with the stucco contractor, matching the color of the brown paper bag that Taylor brought to the site as a sample. The contractor kept adding pigment to the mix until he finally attained the right shade.

A sophisticated rusticity characterized the Auberge interior. In the entrance lobby, Taylor's distinctive concrete and wood window-

Auberge du Soleil. *Top*: Entrance lobby. *Bottom*: Entrance to bar.

pane floor underscored an ash hall table set on diamond-shaped concrete pedestals. The inspiration was the French Baroque game table in his office. Taylor used this model repeatedly throughout his career. He was effusive about the welcoming presence of the table, which, at the Auberge, was usually amplified by a centerpiece of overscaled yellow sunflowers growing out of a heavy antique stone container.

Entrance into the bar was to the right of the hall table, through a wide doorway that followed the curvature of the circular room. Inside, wood-topped bar tables and cane-backed chairs were arranged around a central cider tree, which extended thirty feet up from the floor to the skylit conical ceiling. A pair of recessed leather banquettes framed the fireplace on the north wall.

Taylor always "created as he went along. Each time he came [to the Auberge], there were changes." He insisted on tearing out the south wall of the round room, even though it was nearly completed. The bar was going to be built along this wall, and Taylor wanted it to be windowed. He felt that the view of the valley should be maximized, especially for the patrons who clustered around the bar. Another innovation was to outline the tall encircling ledge of the bar with stacked fire logs. The logs enhanced the organic dimension of the interior, accentuated the height of the room, and directed the eye upward. Unfortunately, they also became a maintenance issue. The logs had to be replaced periodically, which was an arduous task.

Vibrant colors, fresh flowers, and a commanding view of the valley set the tone for the dining room, located on the opposite side of the lobby, across from the bar. Taylor provided the dining room with various seating arrangements. He placed three banquette-lined alcoves along the back wall of the room and furnished the floor with round and square tables of four. Tables were also set up on the connecting terrace, perched above the unspoiled bucolic setting.

The principal source of color in the dining room was the multicolored Indian striped fabric that covered the banquettes. Vibrant red was the dominant color. It was an effective ground for the narrow vertical bands of color, which included luminous shades of orange, pink, purple, blue, and lime green. A Gustavo Rivera oil painting, which hung in one of the alcoves, also infused color into the room.

Auberge du Soleil.
This page: Two views of dining room.
Opposite: Dining terrace.

Black Room,
Auberge du Soleil.

The lower level of the Auberge included two function rooms—the Black Room and the White Room. The Black Room, which was below the bar, followed the same blueprint. Its color scheme was dramatic. Flat black painted walls and natural wood offset shocking-pink ball pillows and glazed black chintz upholstery decorated with a floral print in vibrant reds, pinks, and greens.

Mirrored walls overlaid with narrow strips of custom white lattice characterized the White Room. Here, guests enjoyed private dining at round tables clothed in heavy white cotton. The caned-back dining chairs were also white, but their seats were cushioned in solid shades of hot pink, orange, yellow, and green. Vibrant colors also defined the wool carpet, whose texture and composition of slender stripes resembled an old-fashioned rag rug.

Several years after opening the restaurant, the Rouases initiated the second part of their plan. They asked Taylor and Walker to create nine villas along the sloping hillside of their property. The villas were to contain thirty-six one- and two-bedroom guest suites. Walker's design for the villas was derived from the main building. This consistency created an appropriate transition, both architecturally and environmentally, as the project evolved. It also engendered familiarity for the regular guests who knew the Auberge from its early days.

Taylor was "the ultimate consumer." He had "very definite ideas of what a hotel room should be" and how to pamper a guest. The day before Taylor was to start planning the villas, he met the Rouases "in the entranceway of the Auberge and, pantomiming carrying a suitcase in each hand, said, 'Okay, here I am, your first guest, eager for a week of luxurious relaxation. Where do I go and what do I do next?' Every step and every hour of the way has to be gracious serendipity, or I may not come back again." Sheer comfort and practicality governed Taylor's interior decoration of the villas. Because he "wanted to eliminate the sense that another person had used the room before," Taylor specified built-in furniture, slip-covered upholstery, and brownish-pink Mexican Saltillo tile for the floors, headboards, counters, and side tables. The floor tiles also continued up the sides of the bed and sofa platforms, which eliminated skirting and the need to dust underneath this furniture. The fixed arrangement also enabled "Taylor to control the day-to-day look without operational interpretation." He wanted everything in the rooms to be washable and easy to clean, including the colorful oversized rectangular hooked area rugs, the round ash wood dining tables, and the leather-upholstered *equipales* furniture.

Rich sun-drenched colors pervaded the interiors. Plush Crowder chenille, custom-dyed in solid shades of yellow, orange, and shocking pink, was used for the suites' upholstery, pillows, and bedspreads. A large abstract oil painting by Sigrid Burton also contributed brilliant color and originality to each room. Taylor pioneered the use of original art in hotels. His clients appreciated his foresight when it came to selecting art.

Guest suite, Auberge du Soleil.

Taylor "expected his vision to be executed exactly." He explained to Adair Borba, the Auberge general manager, who worked closely with him during the project, how the rooms should look. Taylor's infinitesimal instructions covered everything, including the positioning, fluffing, and creasing of the pillows. They were to look "beautifully casual, but not haphazardly placed." Taylor also showed Borba how to make the beds. He sized the bedspreads generously, anticipating luxurious fullness in the crease underscoring the pillows, for which he specified three different combinations of stuffing.

The villas, like the restaurant, were an instant success. Taylor's grasp of how the country resort was going to operate created a buzz that traveled around the world. Rouas proudly remembers the day that he lounged by the pool at a Balinese resort, overhearing a couple rave about their daughter's wedding, which was hosted at the Auberge.

The Auberge du Soleil was an excellent calling card for Taylor. Warren (Ned) Spieker Jr., the prominent West Coast developer, was dining at the Auberge du Soleil during the early 1980s, the same time period during which his company was building the Montgomery Washington Tower at the foot of Montgomery Street, in the heart of San Francisco's financial district. Spieker was impressed with the Auberge, which he said had "a great feel." He asked Claude Rouas who

had decorated the restaurant's interiors, getting Taylor's name and telephone number from him. Spieker was looking for an outstanding decorator to design the model apartment at the twenty-six-story tower. The Montgomery Washington Tower was being built with six floors of condominiums on top of twenty floors of office space. It was the first mixed-use building in San Francisco.

Spieker telephoned Taylor a few days after dining at the Auberge and made an appointment to meet him. He invited Taylor to his office, located in the building next door to the tower. Spieker's office shared similar views of the city, Coit Tower, and San Francisco Bay with the prospective model apartment. He wanted Taylor to be keenly aware of them.

Taylor embraced Spieker's project. He enjoyed planning interiors in concert with spectacular views. They were central to his triumphant blueprint for the twenty-fourth-floor two-bedroom apartment, which he amplified with mirrored walls, white travertine floors, and textured materials.

Taylor's relevance to the Montgomery Washington Tower went well beyond Spieker's original intent. Once his plans for the twenty-five-hundred square foot model were solidified, he told Spieker that the decor had to "carry over" into the adjacent elevator hallway serving four additional apartments. Spieker accepted Taylor's assertion, al-

Guest suite, Auberge du Soleil.

lowing him to specify a hall in muted tones and also border its char-coal-gray runner of wool carpet in white travertine. Needless to say, the plan was applied to all six hallways in the residential division of the building.

Taylor also told Spieker that "it just won't do that the elevators and the lobby don't match the halls." This prompted further redesign of the building during its construction. The entire interiors of the lobby and the elevators were sheathed in white travertine.

Taylor's initial changes did not prepare Spieker or Jeff Heller, the architect from the San Francisco firm K/M/D who designed the build-ing, for the penultimate modification to its blueprint. Taylor rejected the tower's intended greenish granite skin because it clashed with the model apartment, even when Spieker told him the stone was already ordered. Taylor backed off from his request nominally, limiting the change to the building's portico and entrance plaza, which he wanted fabricated in white travertine. Regardless, the change of heart was only temporary. Taylor quickly resumed his "audacious and unabashed" demands, telling Spieker that he didn't think it was a good idea to use green travertine at all. He wanted the Montgomery Washington Tower completely redesigned and sheathed exclusively in white travertine, assuring Spieker that "it will sparkle and be a beautiful building," just like the Transamerica Pyramid on the opposite side of Montgomery

Street. Taylor espoused to his client that, together, the two white travertine towers would form the gateway to Montgomery Street. Spieker still thought the request impossible and reminded Taylor that the travertine had already been ordered. Taylor, always resolute to his position, shepherded Spieker to "lots of buildings" in San Francisco, eventually convincing him by example that the change was essential to the success of the tower.

Taylor, accompanied by Spieker's partner, was soon en route to Italy to visit the quarry outside of Milan with which they were deal-ing. Although they were able to cancel the order for the green traver-tine, another major challenge ensued. The travertine for the building was expected in San Francisco in five months, the same amount of time needed to quarry the white stone. Unfortunately, the quarry was about to shut down for the annual August vacation, making it impos-sible to meet the building's firm construction schedule. Taylor perse-vered, asking the quarry foreman what it would take to get the crew to work through the month of August. The foreman told Taylor it was not possible. Taylor, undeterred by the foreman's response, repeated the question to him, finally resulting in the breakthrough he expected. The quarry's eight-person crew agreed to work through the month-long vacation if each of them received their full wages, a bonus, and a brand-new Fiat. The deal was struck, the assignment consummated, and the travertine reached San Francisco on time. Michael Taylor had completed "the biggest slip-covering of his career!"

Taylor's project at the Montgomery Washington Tower coincided with various residential commissions in northern and southern California and on the East Coast. In San Francisco, John and Dodie Rosekrans hired Taylor to decorate their baronial mansion in Pacific Heights, which John thought was "one hell of a house" when Dodie showed it to him for the first time. The Spanish Renaissance–style villa designed by Willis Polk (1867–1924), the prolific San Francisco classicist architect, sat two doors away from their former home. Polk designed the house in 1917 for Andrew and Julia Welch. Julia had willed the house to the Archdiocese of San Francisco when she died in the early 1940s. It served as the archiepiscopal palace for almost four decades. Fortunately, when the Rosekranses purchased the house from the archdiocese in 1979, it was in preserved condition. The house contained at its center a large double-height open atrium with ornately carved sandstone columns, arches, and friezes by Leo Lentelli, the Italian-American sculptor. The scale and monumentality of the project was commensurate with Taylor's own grandiosity. His adroit selection of furniture for the Rosekranses' previous house also suited the new house perfectly, including the upholstered pieces, which had stood the test of time in both quality and design.

The principal rooms—the smoking room, the dining room, and the living room—followed the perimeter of the atrium, which the Rosekranses enclosed with a glass greenhouse roof. The living room opened directly on to the atrium through a balanced pair of tall arched French doors on its south wall, amplifying the generous proportions of the salon and allowing the Rosekranses to entertain in the courtyard year-round, an element that pleased Taylor. Taylor, too, was smitten with the house and, for it, created several of his most legendary interiors.

John and Dodie Rosekrans respected Taylor as both an interior designer and a good friend. John often asked his wife, referring to Taylor, if "she had spoken to God today?" Dodie remembers Taylor as being "outrageous in a way, yet absolutely correct and classical in his work. His taste was infallible and incredible. If he had lived," she said, "he'd have been more wonderful than ever."

In 1982, Alfred and Dede Wilsey hired Taylor to decorate the early twentieth-century Italianate house they had just purchased. Alfred was already a long-standing client of Taylor's. When Dede Wilsey first discussed the plans for her and her husband's new home with "Mikey," she told him, "I don't want a typical Michael Taylor house." Taylor asked, "And what exactly is that?" Wilsey replied, "Oh, you know, white on white, wicker everywhere, huge overstuffed chairs. My feet don't reach the floor. I feel like a pygmy." Wilsey also informed Taylor that she wanted the house to be decorated exclusively in green, yellow, and pink. Although Wilsey's favored color scheme was atypical of Taylor's oeuvre, especially her request for a pink living room, he acquiesced.

Wilsey also asked Taylor to modify the depth of her living room sofa to accommodate her five-foot-three-inch frame. "What?" Taylor asked Wilsey. "Well, good God, I'm going to make you a Michael Taylor sofa. You'll have to get up and sit somewhere else!" When all was said and done, Taylor complied with his client's wishes. At Wilsey's request, he measured her with a tape measure from her hip bone to her knee to ensure the proper depth for the new sofa. Despite the modification, Wilsey complained to Taylor, who was with her when the sofa arrived at the house, that her feet still did not reach the floor when

she sat on the sofa. Wilsey did not like feeling as if she was a guest in her own living room and asked him to fluff it up with another pillow or two. Taylor, unfazed by the comment, told her that she was not sitting right. In the end, Taylor's audaciousness did not overrule Wilsey's perseverance. He made the extra pillows for the sofa.

In 1984, the Wilseys decided to add a garden room to their house. The room, which took eighteen months to build, was to better accommodate the grand holiday party that they hosted every December. The Wilseys always tented their terrace for the party. However, one year the tent blew over just before the party was to begin. The new garden room enclosed the terrace that overlooked San Francisco Bay and the Marin hills. The addition expanded the house and eliminated the threat of a repeat calamity. Robert Swatt, the Bay area architect, drew up the original plans. They were executed by Porter and Steinwedell.

Again, Taylor's input was fundamental to the success of the project. Initially, the garden room was going to be sited at the terrace level. However, Taylor insisted that the room should be built on a higher plane in order to optimize the view. Although Taylor was not concerned about the additional expense that would be required to raise the room, he still had to convince Al Wilsey about the wisdom of the strategy.

Taylor was very clever. One day, while meeting with the Wilseys on their terrace, he held Dede up in the air during Al's brief absence. Taylor wanted her to see how much better the view would be from a higher elevation. He succeeded. When Al returned to the terrace and glimpsed the uncanny exercise, he asked Taylor and his wife, "What are you doing?" Dede replied, "We're decorating." To which Al questioned, "From where?" Although Dede was sure that Wilsey would tell her just to buy higher heels in order to capture the view, he eventually consented. The garden room was built eighteen inches above the terrace level.

Wilsey conceded to "Michael Taylor White" in the garden room because she knew that any other color would fade. *Ficus Benjamina* trees and flowers adorned the expansive, glass-walled room. A touch of a switch controlled the opening of the center skylight in the glass ceiling. Initially, Taylor criticized Al's suggestion of the open roof, "but once he saw it, he took full credit" for the idea. An off-white marble floor and two corbelled walls completed the neutral backdrop in the room. The walls were original to the exterior of the house. However, when the addition was built, Taylor embellished them. He commissioned two Italian plasterers to rusticate the walls. It took them seven months of painstaking artistry to complete the project.

Taylor's health was declining during his work on the Wilsey garden room. Michael Taylor Designs also experienced a major change. Dennis Buchner, the executive vice president of Michael Taylor Designs, decided to pursue other design opportunities. He gave his notice to Taylor. The idea of Buchner's successor "came up over dinner at Russell MacMasters's house." MacMasters knew Paul Weaver, who was vice president of marketing for McGuire, the furniture company. He recommended him to Taylor for the position. At Taylor's request, Buchner interviewed Weaver. On Buchner's recommendation, Taylor hired Weaver for the position. Buchner for his part agreed to remain on staff for several months to assist in the transition. In August 1985, after Buchner had left, Taylor and Weaver formed a corporation, Michael Taylor Designs, Inc., to continue the existing furniture business. They would expand their marketing and develop new products and product lines. According to the agreement between Taylor and

Weaver, this new entity was to be "sole and separate from Taylor's design business."

Taylor's prominence in the field of interior design intensified exponentially during the mid-1980s. He received the American Society of Interior Designers' "Designer of Distinction" award. He was also inducted into *Interior Design* magazine's Interior Design Hall of Fame. The magazine established the award in 1985 "to honor outstanding designers working in the field." Taylor was feted, along with fourteen residential and commercial interior designers and architects, at the first annual awards gala, which was held at the Waldorf-Astoria Hotel in New York. Several good friends and clients, including Jeanne Jackson and Woody and Suzanne Haynes, accompanied him to the celebratory dinner. Taylor's interior design business continued to flourish during this period. He was working on several houses in San Francisco and on the Peninsula.

In San Francisco, one of his most challenging commissions came from Gorham and Diana Knowles. The Knowleses' second house in Presidio Heights was the fourth commission that Taylor undertook for them. He had known Diana for thirty years. She and Taylor had "great fun together." Knowles stimulated Taylor's creativity, which always resulted in close collaborations between the client and the designer. "After working so often together, Michael Taylor and Diana had an idyllic, almost rhapsodic friendship." Taylor and Knowles loved to shop together. Occasionally she disagreed with his choices. When this happened, Taylor always called Knowles in the evening after spending a long day with her to try and convince her to change her mind. Knowles would tell Taylor, "You can talk to me all night and I'm not going to change my mind. I know what I like and what I don't like." He would eventually give up.

The Knowleses' Jackson Street house, although "graceful and charming," was too small for their socially active lifestyle. "They had been looking for a larger house for several years." The couple often entertained at home. They wanted to be able to comfortably host two hundred guests for cocktails or thirty for a seated dinner in their dining room. The mid-1920s house that they purchased in 1980 had no architectural character. However, Diana "envisioned a new-old palace rising" from its foundation.

Before the Knowleses began the complex renovation and remodeling of the house, they allowed it to be used for the 1981 San Francisco Decorator Showcase. When the month-long benefit was over, Diana and Gorham hired Porter and Steinwedell to execute the architectural drawings. It would take five arduous years to transform the house into a classical French villa.

The new floor plan circulated graciously. On the first floor, an impressive travertine-floored entrance gallery flowed into the sitting area, the formal living room, and the newly built skylit garden room, which enclosed the original front garden. Double doors in carved ash opened from the sitting area into the reconfigured formal dining room. A monumental stone staircase at the far end of the gallery led to the second floor. Here, an intimate sitting area introduced the library and the Knowles's master bedroom suite. The library, with its large bay window overlooking Washington Street, was inspired by the Knowleses' former house. Most of the furniture from the Jackson Street library was readapted for the new library.

The Knowleses' master bedroom suite balanced the library. The suite included a sleeping alcove, a sitting area, a study, and his-and-hers dressing rooms and bathrooms. Taylor covered the walls of the entire bedroom, including the alcove ceiling, in muted pink floral chintz. The upholstered headboard, bedspread, and bed skirt were also fabricated in the same material. Originally, Knowles disapproved of the "garish" chintz, but when Taylor reversed it, she allowed him to use it.

Porter and Steinwedell, at their clients' request, transformed the attic into a pair of guestrooms. They created a graceful skylit circular staircase that connected the second floor with the guest quarters. Dormer windows were cut into the pitched roof, expanding the space available for the two cozy bedrooms.

Another of Taylor's major projects came from John and Frances Bowes. The Boweses were long-standing clients and friends of Taylor's, and they commissioned him to decorate the late-1930s Art Deco townhouse they had purchased in 1985 on Russian Hill. The four-story masonry house boasted a one-hundred-and-eighty-degree view of San Francisco Bay. But the house required gutting and remodeling. The Boweses hired Sandy Walker to collaborate with Taylor. The Boweses' project took two and a half years to complete. It resulted in an understated but highly sophisticated interior.

The Boweses' townhouse was one of Taylor's last major commissions. He died from AIDS on June 3, 1986, in the midst of working on the assignment and just as the Wilsey garden room was being finished. He was fifty-nine. The Knowleses' commission and several others were immobilized by Taylor's death.

Michael Taylor's funeral was held on Thursday, June 5, 1986, at Grace Cathedral on Nob Hill. The late-morning service, which was conducted with the pomp and circumstance of a State funeral, drew both a national and an international set of mourners. Attendance reached standing-room capacity. The people who paid their respects to Taylor were "a broad spectrum of individuals whose lives had been touched by him—the Hollywood elite, wealthy clients, benefactors, as well as members of the trade." It was a gathering of "very beautiful people, predominantly male."

Russell MacMasters eulogized Taylor. "The silence was deafening as he approached the podium" before Taylor's heavy bronze casket, lavishly swathed in an overpowering blanket of white carnations "precisely stitched together with red roses" that swept the cathedral's impenetrable Indiana limestone floor. MacMasters's magnificently composed and heartfelt delivery spoke of his dear and longtime friend. "We were the lucky ones who knew Michael and could experience the thrill of divine inspiration, of genius. . . . We also experienced firsthand his exhilarating creative energy . . . a force that reached around the globe in his lifetime and that will long continue to inspire creative people everywhere."

MacMasters's tribute to Taylor acknowledged that "genius is not always compassionate. To resist Michael's creative power was taking on Goliath." He "was tough . . . a difficult friend" and "relentlessly critical of the mundane, of the clichéd, intolerant of the mediocre, and yet devastatingly self-effacing and funny." He "could talk like Baby Snooks and make me laugh so hard, I cried, and yet inspire me to work harder than I ever thought possible. The rewards of sharing his great sensitivity and wit have been stunning gifts for us all."

The loss of Michael Taylor deeply affected his friends, his clients, his associates, and even his estranged mother and half-brother. It riveted the international design world. His death was chronicled extensively. The *New York Times*, *Time*, and *Newsweek* joined the multitude of West Coast newspapers and national design magazines that memorialized him and commemorated his formidable contributions to the field of interior design. Paige Rense, editor of *Architectural Digest*, articulated Taylor's influence succinctly when she wrote that "Michael

The Estate of Michael Taylor auction catalogue.

changed the way we lived. He blasted through the reverence and formality so prevalent in design years ago and brought nature indoors." He "made decorating history. Whatever he did, or didn't do, made news."

Unfortunately, Taylor's death left a great deal of unfinished business in both his personal and his professional lives. Except for Taylor's American Express bill (on which he charged his clothing), which he always paid on time, even when it was sixty thousand dollars in just one month, his financial affairs were in incomprehensible disarray. When he died, he was over three million dollars in debt. Before his death, he asked Alfred Wilsey to serve as the executor of his estate. Taylor respected Wilsey, who was a successful businessman with the savvy and the acumen to conquer the multitude of challenges that ensued with Taylor's financial affairs. The obstacles included the contesting of Taylor's will—on the grounds of undue influence—by Grace Paxton. Taylor's adored and generous relationship with his octogenarian mother "had soured in recent years" before his death.

Taylor's interior design business was the first order of concern in Wilsey's strategic agenda. He made the business solvent, advancing it the substantial amount of capital needed in order for it to complete Taylor's unfinished jobs. Wilsey worked closely with Suzanne Tucker and Timothy Marks. Marks had been the firm's valued expeditor since 1983. It took them one year to accomplish this task.

Wilsey, along with an attorney he hired on a full-time basis, also tackled the receivables and payables of the business. They wanted to ensure an effective cash flow and the timely payment of all expenditures. This included repossessing the inventory that was on approval with Taylor's clients. Each client was expected to pay for their loaned piece immediately or return it to Taylor's estate. His interior design operation was being run in a businesslike manner for the first time.

Wilsey and his counsel decided to auction all of Taylor's posses-

sions in an attempt to satisfy his debts. They chose the San Francisco headquarters of Butterfield & Butterfield, California's preeminent auction house, which was established in 1865 and was owned by Barney Osher. Kenneth Winslow, Butterfield's director of furniture and decorative arts at the time, led the team that organized the auction. Winslow and his San Francisco associates spent four weeks cataloging Taylor's possessions at the Sea Cliff house. Every day, ten to fifteen associates from every department at Butterfield scoured the house from top to bottom. They inventoried in excess of twenty-five hundred items, which composed more than fourteen hundred lots in the auction. A good deal of Taylor's property was illustrated in *The Estate of Michael Taylor*, a handsomely composed 222 page hardbound catalogue that Butterfields published for the occasion. The much-sought-after auction catalogue, the first hardbound copy in the history of Butterfields (at Wilsey's suggestion), sold for twenty dollars.

The principal sale of Michael Taylor's property was scheduled for April 7 through April 9, 1987. Although the one-year anniversary of his death was fast approaching, the passage of time had not assuaged the fervent mourning that Taylor's friends, clients, and business associates suffered. Chili Kohlenberg, one of Taylor's long-standing San Francisco clients, said that "she wouldn't consider hiring anyone else." Taylor had been going to redo her master bedroom for the second time in twenty-two years, but when Kohlenberg "heard of his death," she was "having everything in the bedroom copied as a living tribute to Michael." She planned "to live happily in that white monotone bedroom for another twenty-two years."

For the bereaved, the Butterfield auction once again commemorated the life and accomplishments of Taylor. On the evening of March 31, 1987, the Fine Arts Museums of San Francisco hosted a "Tribute to Michael Taylor" at the auction house. The invitation-only cocktail reception benefited the museums and was limited to six hundred guests. This was the first exhibition of Taylor's collection. The event tribute committee was chaired by Dodie Rosekrans and was composed of nineteen women who were clients and good friends of Taylor's.

Butterfields staged Taylor's furnishings superbly in eight room settings and twenty-seven groupings, which replicated their placement in his house. Hoards of visitors pored over the vignettes during the five days of public viewing that preceded the three-day auction. The auction itself had four distinct sessions. The crowd marveled at Taylor's monumental four-poster bed, which stood at the entrance to the auction. It sold for twenty thousand dollars.

The auction, which drew standing-room crowds of up to one thousand attendees, was staggering. It was a huge social event that was covered by the San Francisco press. "The room had real energy and buzz, more like a big party than an auction. There was scarcely a decorator of any note from California, southern or northern, who wasn't there, and more than a few from the East Coast." The first four rows of seating were roped off for designated guests, which included the committee members of the preview party.

Taylor's property sold very well. He was so well regarded and his collections were so unique and interesting that everyone yearned for a piece of "Saint Michael." During the first session, the bidders purchased furniture, sculpture, and porcelains at prices that well exceeded the all-inclusive pre-auction estimate of one million four hundred thousand dollars. The provenances of these treasures, which included the highly coveted bronze works of Diego Giacometti, were diverse. They symbolized the singularity of Taylor's taste.

Invitation to *A Tribute to Michael Taylor*.

The second session of the auction began with the sale of Taylor's two cars—a 1979 black Porsche 928 and a 1976 sable Rolls Royce Corniche two-door hardtop. Taylor loved sexy and luxurious automobiles. From his earliest days in business, he always dashed around town in sleek and fastidiously detailed models. His jet-black 1959 limited-edition Cadillac Eldorado Biarritz convertible, with its "rapier-sharp tailfins" and bullet-shaped front bumper, was an indelible fixture alongside the curb at 556 Sutter Street.

The last session of the auction featured Taylor's clothing, jewelry, books, houseplants, and orchids. The vast inventory of clothing was especially overwhelming. It reflected Taylor's favorite pastime. Every Saturday, Taylor shopped at Wilkes Bashford in San Francisco. He often purchased the same article of clothing in duplicate and in multiple fabrics and colors. When Taylor died, he had not worn many of the clothes that filled his large walk-in closets. The price tags still dangled from them as they were auctioned. The trendy apparel included four-dozen outerwear jackets, eighteen of which were designed by Claude Montana. Taylor was especially smitten with Montana's black leather jackets (the auction included nine of them), which he also purchased in solid shades of red, yellow, and green. At his death, he owned one model of every jacket that Montana designed.

Taylor's jewelry was also a big hit. The ninety-odd pieces included rings, bracelets, cuff links, necklaces, and twelve wristwatches. Taylor collected wristwatches—Audemar Piguet, Cartier, Porsche-design, and Rolex. When he dressed in one of his characteristic ways, with his shirtsleeves rolled up, there was often a watch on each wrist.

Butterfields auctioned Taylor's "less pricey" property on April 14, 1987. The sale was held at Butterfields–Utah Street, the auction house's warehouse. There were hundreds of eager bidders and curiosity seekers who crowded into the vast building. The thousand lots of property that were offered for sale came principally from Taylor's warehouses and included additional clothing, furniture, decorative arts, architectural fragments and moldings, and barrels full of infinite yardages of cotton, linen, and silk fabrics. Everything sold at the adjunct auction, including Taylor's signature collection of dark-brown leather handle bags that he had custom made as carryalls for fabric samples. The oversized bags, which were monogrammed and outfitted with swanky brass hardware, were reminiscent of a physician's valise.

The estate of Michael Taylor was the largest and most successful single-owner auction in the history of Butterfields. It brought in more than three and a half million dollars, exclusive of all commissions. The triumphant results—along with the sale of Taylor's house, his interior design business to Tucker and Marks, and Michael Taylor Designs, Inc., to Weaver—enabled Wilsey to satisfy all of the estate's outstanding debts and loans. He also established, with residual funds, the Michael Taylor Trust, which advances the decorative arts in the Bay area. Paxton was compensated, too. She received, by the ruling of a San Francisco Superior Court judge, a substantial portion of Taylor's estate, the bulk of which came from his life insurance policy.

Michael Taylor was "the James Dean of decorators: the innovative one. An original." Always the renegade, he was curtly dismissive of the copyists whom he labeled as unimaginative "bleeders, followers, and leeches." His contributions to interior design spanned three decades and influenced interiors internationally. While the majority of his commissions were residential, he also decorated hotels, stores, restaurants, clubhouses, and even several freighters. The interiors included here, ranging from the classical tradition to the "California Look," give a broad picture of the range and inimitable accomplishments of Taylor's career. The sequence is chronological.

MR. AND MRS. EVERETT W. TURNER

MODESTO, CALIFORNIA, 1956

Everett and Mabel Turner commissioned William Wilson Wurster (1895–1973), the influential Bay Area architect, to design a contemporary brick ranch-style house in 1941. Although the Modesto house was handsomely decorated at the time, the Turners asked Taylor, fifteen years later, to refresh and lighten its interiors.

Mabel Turner knew Taylor when he was growing up in Modesto, an agricultural hub in the fertile San Joaquin Valley. She "spotted" his talent early in his career. The Turner job was Taylor's first personal commission. It occurred while he was transitioning from his small shop on Post Street to his new space on Sutter Street.

Taylor informed the Turners "that his approach would be fresh, exuberant, and natural." First, he stripped and bleached all of the interiors' floors and paneling, which were originally very dark and uncomplimentary to "Mrs. Turner's immaculate style" and "the architectural detailing of Mr. Wurster." Taylor's experimentation with the pure and airy tableau was the springboard for his innovative and pioneering "California Look."

LIVING ROOM

The monochromatic backdrop was especially effective in the Turners' living room, where the principal seating area was arranged around the clean-lined travertine fireplace. The balanced plan consisted of a pair of sofas and four Louis XVI cane-backed fauteuils that were aligned individually with the corners of the coffee table. Although the table and the sofas were purposely overscaled for the room, Taylor's adroit color palette made them visually weightless. The natural finish of the oak and travertine table, and the parchment linen velvet covering the sofas, blended fluidly with the room's bleached redwood paneling.

Taylor accessorized the living room with several of his signature pieces. He placed one of a pair of white plaster Giacometti-style rope lamps on each side of the fireplace and a cow-skin rug on the bleached oak floor. However, the living room's pièce de résistance was the flourishing fishtail palm tree, which Taylor told his client was unavailable in California. Mabel Turner, undeterred by that minor detail, had one "'smuggled' in from Florida, airfreighted in a carpet packing tube."

LIBRARY

Taylor anchored the library with several pieces of period furniture that he bought from Frances Elkins's business estate. They included the lit de repos and the French provincial armoire, which he integrated comfortably with a pair of Syrie Maugham tufted armchairs and ottomans. Although Taylor acquiesced to dark finishes on the library's wood pieces, he maintained a monochromatic sensibility in the room. The pale tobacco linen that covered the French sofa, the chairs, the ottomans and the walls gently dominated the interior. The library's Taylor-designed white plaster bean-jar lamps validated his admiration of Alberto Giacometti (1901–1966) and his brother Diego Giacometti (1902–1985). They were Swiss sculptors who designed original lamps and additional fixtures for Jean-Michel Frank (1895–1941), the French interior decorator and furniture designer.

DINING ROOM

The Turner dining room exemplified Taylor's prescient taste and his gift for placing exquisite antiques against a clean and pared-down backdrop. The seventeenth-century coromandel screen, the French dining table and chairs and the eighteenth-century bronze doré rock-crystal chandelier were not customary in an interior of such sparseness. Neither was the fishtail palm tree that soared toward the dining table and the pair of flower-laden English blackamoor containers accessorizing the table. Several of the antiques in the dining room came from Rose Cumming (1887–1968), the legendary proprietress of a decorating and antiques shop in New York. Taylor adored the eccentric Cumming and her exceptional but quirky taste. Although he patronized her Upper East Side shop often, he wasn't able to persuade her to part with everything that he "had to have" of her treasured inventory.

MASTER BEDROOM

Taylor created a crisp and subtly textured patina in the Turners' master bedroom. He dressed the room's pair of tall, to-the-ceiling canopy beds in off-white diamond-quilted linen and incorporated two Giacometti-style plaster lamps and a travertine fireplace into the decor. The neutral setting also welcomed a diverse selection of antiques. They included a pair of Louis XV tête-à-tête chairs, an eighteenth-century marquetry-topped French bouillotte table and an English bedside table. The room's eclecticism was enhanced by the sixteenth-century Spanish oil painting that hung above the fireplace.

MR. AND MRS. THOMAS L. KEMPNER

NEW YORK, NEW YORK, 1956

Nan Kempner and Michael Taylor were long-standing friends. Irma Schlesinger, Kempner's mother, was one of Taylor's early San Francisco clients and greatest mentors. He worked on the interior design of the Schlesingers' Pacific Heights townhouse after the death of Frances Elkins, the Schlesingers' original decorator.

Kempner and her husband, Thomas Kempner, hired Taylor in 1956 to decorate the Park Avenue duplex in New York that they had just purchased. Kempner started planning for the apartment when she ran into Taylor while vacationing in Palm Springs. After she described the apartment to Taylor, he told her that he wanted to do it. Kempner accepted Taylor's offer, and the two of them abandoned the desert for San Francisco.

Taylor and Kempner, aided with the floor plan of the duplex, planned the entire layout of her and her husband's new home in Taylor's office. They even decided on "the shapes of the banquettes for her drawing room with string outlines on the [office] floor."

DRAWING ROOM

The duplex's drawing room, while it was a repository for a collection of rare antiques, defied tradition. Irma Schlesinger scoffed at the room's pair of deep oversized tufted banquettes and their accompanying elongated ottomans. The Taylor-designed pieces, upholstered in creamy-beige narrow-wale cotton corduroy, reminded her of a bordello—not a salon!

Taylor's design for the drawing room created comfort and relaxed casualness amid a backdrop of formal elegance. A twelve-panel coromandel screen stood, partially folded, against the room's principal wall, and a muted monochromatic Aubusson carpet covered the ebonized wood floor. Impressionistic art, antique English mirrors, and a suite of Italian open armchairs with carved gold-gilt rope and tassel frames contributed additional pedigree to the room. Kempner said that after the drawing room was completed, "every decorator in town tried to come in and knock it off," despite the fact that the enormous banquettes and ottomans had to be "hoisted through the [Kempners'] window."

DINING ROOM

In the dining room, eighteenth-century hand-painted Chinese silk panels, "which depicted birds and butterflies flitting in and out of grafted trees tied with ribbons," complemented Kempner's collection of Oriental export and early Meissen porcelain birds. The china birds, which she collected in pairs, were arranged throughout the faux-wood-grain painted room that Taylor furnished with an English dining table, eighteenth-century chairs, and a multicolored French needlepoint carpet. The crystal chandelier, which glowed with authentic candlelight, was Anglo-Irish.

GUEST ROOM

Taylor also covered the walls of the Kempners' guest room in antique Chinese wallpaper. The wallpaper, which was removed from Irma Schlesinger's master bedroom after her death, depicted an idyllic garden scene handpainted on a ground of coral. The room's pair of white-washed Syrie Maugham Regency tester beds, with their soft coral-hued drapery, spreads, and skirting, amplified the decor's Far Eastern influence. The diminutive wooden bells that outlined the bed's scalloped wood crown cornice added charm to the room, the restful hue of which had been influenced in part by one of Dodie Rosekrans's long coral necklaces.

MR. AND MRS. JOHN S. LOGAN

HILLSBOROUGH, CALIFORNIA, 1957

LIVING ROOM

When Taylor decorated for John and Elizabeth Logan in 1957, he bathed their living room in a cheerful palette of yellow and warm white. He covered the majority of the room's upholstered pieces in a hand-blocked sunflower print and draped its windows in vibrant yellow cotton. The curtains—which contributed the greatest concentration of color to the interior—were dramatized by their copiously white-fringed cascading panels. The mixture of the avant-garde Giacometti-style plaster lamps with a modicum of traditional pieces also complemented Taylor's design for the room.

In 1974, the Logans asked Taylor to update the living room, even though they had enjoyed it thoroughly for seventeen years. Fortunately, the room functioned well, "so there was no need to change the arrangement" or the furniture. The transformation applied only to "color and pattern." The original upholstery was replaced with Brunschwig & Fils quilted white cotton whose imaginative botanical print was patterned predominantly in vibrant strawberry red and green. The curtains, which were changed to solid strawberry cotton, were simplified from their previous design. Although Taylor repeated the box cornice in his new rendition, he specified panels that were exclusively straight-line. Their enhancement came from the trimming of white linen-and-cotton braid.

The Logans' living room appeared in *House & Garden* in September 1957. It was the lead photograph in a feature entitled "Color Comes First." Faber Birren, *House & Garden*'s color consultant at the time, wrote the article. He stated that Taylor's use of "warm whites spiked with yellow" related the living room to "its garden vista."

House & Garden also highlighted the Logans' living room in their October 1974 feature "Color Magic." In the article, several of America's top decorators—including Taylor—advised the magazine's readers "how to make a room more inviting by *keeping the best, updating the rest*." The story, which also articulated that "one touch of today could be all you need to give your favorite room a lift," validated its viewpoint with side-by-side photographs of Taylor's alternate designs for the Logans.

MR. AND MRS. HERBERT W. RICHARDS

WOODSIDE, CALIFORNIA, 1957

GUEST ROOM

Taylor created an enchanting guest room for
Herb and Peggy Richards. He anchored the
bedroom with a pair of his favorite Syrie
Maugham Regency tester beds and an Indian
white painted hardwood settee. The beds were
draped and outfitted in white organdy embroidered with red strawberries, green stems, and
leaves. Taylor accompanied these with Austrian
curtains and tufted Maugham armchairs.
The walls, which were painted to match the
embroidery, put the finishing touches on
the room's overall delicate pattern.

LIVING ROOM

The Richardses' living room was influenced by
Taylor's design for the Kempners' apartment.
He specified a pair of large ottomans to flank
the fireplace in the spacious California salon.
Although the tufted ottomans were unconventional on the West Coast, they integrated
successfully with the room's pair of Syrie
Maugham roll-arm sofas and armchairs, which
were upholstered in putty Belgian linen corduroy.
The mélange of antiques—English, Venetian,
and Chinese—along with zebra-skin rugs,
enhanced the distinctiveness and sophistication
of one of Taylor's early assignments.

Taylor was especially proud of the Richards
house. One afternoon in the late 1950s, he telephoned Peggy Richards from San Francisco to
tell her that he was on his way to Woodside.
He wanted to "stop by" with a friend to show
him the house. When Peggy Richards asked
Taylor who he was bringing, he asked her to
wait until they arrived to find out. Taylor soon
appeared at the Richardses' front door with Rock
Hudson. Their spur-of-the-moment visit was
a startling surprise to Herb and Peggy Richards
and to Kathy Richards, the Richardses' five-year-
old daughter. She was so "beside herself" on
seeing Hudson in the front hall of the house
"that she dropped her dolly" on the floor.
Hudson, the ever-so-charming movie-star legend,
bent down, picked up the doll, and returned
it to his young admirer.

MR. AND MRS. BROOKS WALKER

SAN FRANCISCO, CALIFORNIA, 1958

Brooks and Marjory Walker commissioned Taylor to decorate the shingle-style hillside house that they built during the late 1950s. Joseph Esherick (1914–1998), the Bay Area architect and one of the cofounders of the College of Environmental Design at the University of California, Berkeley, designed the Russian Hill house. Esherick, like Taylor, was sympathetic to organic design.

LIVING ROOM

The Walkers asked Taylor to create a country atmosphere in the new house even though they had recently moved from the Peninsula into the city. He succeeded by bringing nature indoors. White and grassy-green fabrics, the clear lacquered finish of the ponderosa pine walls, and profuse natural light composed a garden setting inside the Walkers' traditionally furnished living room year-round. The room's twin love seats were covered in printed cotton twill. Green Belgian linen trimmed the white duck curtains, which were tied back to frame a view of the landscape. The glass-roofed solarium bay in the living room also enhanced the out-of-doors indoors sensibility.

MASTER BEDROOM

When the editors of *House & Garden* presented their portfolio of "romantic beds" to their readership in 1959, the Walkers' master bedroom was foremost on the list. They wrote, "The bedroom, too long a bare chamber, is getting a new graceful dress inspired by fashion's Empire Look."

Taylor's design for the Walkers' bedroom restored "this grand tradition." He outfitted the room exclusively in one fabric. Toile de Jouy, in restful blue and white, was used for the bed hangings, the bedspreads, and the window treatments. The elegant fabric was also the appropriate foil for the bedroom's traditional furniture, including the large gilded Baroque mirror that hung above the bureau.

MR. AND MRS. ALBERT E. SCHLESINGER

ATHERTON, CALIFORNIA, 1958

Al and Irma Schlesinger maintained a weekend house in Atherton, California. The house was a welcome respite from city living. It also solved the predicament of where to install Al Schlesinger's hunting trophies and the panoply of sizable stuffed game that he hunted down on his frequent African safaris. Irma Schlesinger, who ascertained that her husband's prized possessions would be inappropriate in their Pacific Heights townhouse, relegated them to the Peninsula house.

LIVING ROOM

Irma Schlesinger's clear-cut decisiveness created a unique springboard for Taylor's striking interior decoration of the country house. In the living room, Taylor specified red-and-pink striped Mexican cotton for the upholstery and the pair of fixed panels flanking the room's principal sofa. The panels, which suggested the profile of a coromandel screen, framed a boldly graphic maasai shield and a pair of crossed African spears that were inventively mounted to the wall behind the sofa.

Black was the perfect accent color in the living room. Its confident hue related to the shield, the spears, and the diverse Africana that accessorized the interior. The color also dictated Taylor and Schlesinger's selection of furniture for the room. The eclectic mixture of pieces included French provincial ladder-back chairs, a Queen Anne japanned chioiserie secretary, and eighteenth-century dining chairs that Taylor stained black. The zebra-skin rugs, which were arranged on the soft putty stained hardwood floor, also flattered the room's design scheme. Schlesinger, who was renowned for her great taste and style, understood the essence of Taylor's practiced design, in spite of the fact that they often fought like cats and dogs over design decisions. Schlesinger operated "on the principle that if each thing is beautiful in itself, its period is irrelevant."

MR. AND MRS. MICHAEL RYAN

WOODSIDE, CALIFORNIA, 1960

LIVING ROOM

The nucleus of the Ryans' Woodside house was its living room. The living room was spacious, and its generous proportions allowed Taylor to create a hospitable gathering place for the Ryan family and their friends. The principal seating, which consisted of a pair of comfortable sofas and a fireside bench, was all slipcovered in white duck. The pieces were symmetrically arranged around a low but wide contemporary fireplace. A natural-colored goat's-hair rug anchored the seating area, and a balanced pair of small round *equipales* tables—which harmonized with the room's French provincial secretary and Giacometti-style plaster lamps—fronted each of the sofas. Two groupings of chairs, strategically placed, provided additional seating.

SUNROOM, READING NOOK

SUNROOM

The feeling of spaciousness in the living room was amplified by the light-filled sunroom that Taylor created from the original traditionally appointed library. Following the profile of the only windowed wall in the room, Taylor replaced two bookcase-lined walls with mullioned floor-to-ceiling glass interspersed with narrow divisions of trellis hung in ivy. The transformation of the room was miraculous. Taylor not only expanded the visual and physical perimeters of the room but also integrated it with the bucolic setting of the Ryans' property, which included a graceful waterfall and a hillside landscape that Taylor lined with a profusion of azaleas in his signature white. The distinction between indoors and outdoors was practically nonexistent. Taylor "always fantasized that you lived outdoors in your house."

The predominantly white duck slip-covered furniture in the sunroom—a generously scaled sofa and several comfortable armchairs—perpetuated the openness of the room. Although a firm proponent of the white-on-white color scheme, Taylor skillfully eluded the risk of creating a monotonous interior. His inclusion of lush plants and various textures (in this room a calfskin rug, which anchored the seating area; Giacometti-style plaster lighting fixtures; a pair of round *equipales* side tables, sprayed glossy white; and a tall Baroque white-pattern-on-white ceramic stove) added additional dimension to the room.

MRS. MARYON DAVIES LEWIS

GALLERY

Taylor specified a neutral palette for Lewis's thirty-foot-long gallery, which swept from the front door, past the main staircase and the dining room, before terminating at the entrance to the living room. He anchored the fourteen-foot-tall hallway with a white-fringed cream and white Moroccan runner, one of the many pieces of select inventory that he purchased from Frances Elkins's business estate. The runner was a superb choice for the gallery. Its geometrically patterned design, although defined by subtle hues, contributed a tactile and textural quality to the sizable space. Using the runner as a foundation, Taylor painted the gallery walls in eggshell mixed with a touch of red. Taylor was fanatical about his paint and, when necessary, he communicated with his painter directly, over the telephone from wherever he was in the world and at any hour of the day or night depending on the time zone he was in, giving detailed instructions on how to properly mix the selected colors.

Taylor selected a monumental console table, appropriately scaled, for the gallery. He placed the table, fabricated completely in putty and sienna-veined marble, against the wall opposite the staircase. The eight-foot-long table, with its substantial pair of legs and block feet, underscored an ornately framed antique Venetian wall mirror. The installation of the console table, as was customary for Taylor, was no easy feat. The large piece required a group of brawny movers to carry it from the moving van into the house and through the long gallery where, under Taylor's infinitesimally explicit and nerve-wracking direction, it was coddled and installed with the respect and consideration befitting a piece of classical sculpture.

DINING ROOM

Brunschwig & Fils Jacobean documentary
chintz printed in red, raspberry, green, and blue
on cream ground enlivened Lewis's dining room.
Taylor's selection of furniture for the room—
French provincial cane-backed dining chairs,
a Waterford crystal chandelier, and a subtly
textured winter-white rug—illustrated his ability
at mixing varied periods and styles. As he had
done in the living room, Taylor also heightened
the dining room by installing the curtains and
woven blinds at the ceiling's cornice line.
An engaging view into the house's connecting
card room amplified the parameters of the
dining room.

LIVING ROOM

The neutral background of Lewis's gallery set the
tone for Taylor's interior decoration of her capacious living room, which, before his arrival on
the scene, was dark, grim, and lined with floor-
to-ceiling zebrawood bookcases. Taylor insisted
on ripping out the built-in bookcases, instruct-
ing Lewis in his compelling voice that she was
not going to "live like a bachelor" in her new
house. Once the bookcases were removed, Taylor began transforming the living room into an
elegant and cosmopolitan interior. He upholstered the living room walls and two sofas in
pearl gray Brunschwig & Fils embossed linen
velvet. The imported and decoratively patterned
fabric was luxurious and embracing, especially
after Lewis suggested to Taylor that he soften its
inherent stiffness by running it through an in-
dustrial dryer at the St. Francis Hotel. The focal
point of the living room, with the exception of
its auspicious and commanding view of San
Francisco Bay, was its outstanding antique Turk-
ish Oushak carpet, which Taylor had purchased
at a Paris showroom. Taylor drew the principal

accent color for the room, raspberry, from the carpet, whose bone ground was also complemented by restful shades of celadon and pale gray.

The boldest statement of raspberry came from the window covering, a phrase that Taylor used insistently because he deplored the word "drapes." Sumptuously gathered tieback curtains in raspberry velvet, which were lined in heavy pale-gray silk taffeta, anchored the principal oversized picture window and each mullioned window that was nestled into three of the room's corners. Taylor specified that the curtains should hang from the room's cornice line, suggesting ceiling-high windows, and puddle on the floor as if "the lady had too long a skirt." He also selected for each window beige bamboo blinds with an abbreviated drop. These tempered the glare from the Bay and infused an organic dimension into the more formal collection of rare French, Chinese, and Venetian furnishings and accessories.

MARCH

House & Garden

60¢

Fresh inspiration for your planning and decorating

Sunshine colors to make your house sparkle

Thirty wonderful ideas for your windows

How to find space

A greenhouse to live in

COOKBOOK: SOUP-AND-SALAD SUPPERS

MASTER BEDROOM

Taylor and Lewis's adventuresome taste also materialized in Lewis's master bedroom. The centerpiece of the bedroom, Lewis's canopy bed, also enthralled *House & Garden*, which featured the bedroom on their March 1967 cover. The bed, with its overwhelmingly striking canopy lavishly draped in luscious shades of pink and green silk taffeta, was inspired by Rose Cumming (1887–1968), the legendary interior design innovator. Taylor combined the draping designs of Cumming's own canopy bed in her Manhattan townhouse and that of her mother's lit à la polonaise, also in Cumming's house, to create the blueprint for Lewis's bed. It took several hours for Taylor and his assistant to drape the taffeta on Lewis's bed. They started at the crown of the canopy, shirring the vibrant sections of taffeta

"onto a rectangular steel frame, covering completely the curved steel arms and the straight posts at the corners of the bed that supported it." Taylor, who adored trim, arranged the taffeta into a copious bouquet of pink and green pouf rosettes at the top of each post, crowning the vertical span of the multicolored draping that dropped gracefully to the bedroom floor. Lewis, to this day, has preserved her canopy bed, remembering with amusement her mother's initial reaction upon seeing it for the first time. Louise Davies asked her daughter, "Just who do you think you are?" Lewis also remembers poignantly Taylor telling her at the outset of decorating her house, "When I finish this house, Maryon, I want you to be able to grow old here."

CARD ROOM

The most radical departure from tradition in Lewis's house was Taylor's decoration of her card room. The room sat, in balance to the living room, at the forefront of the gallery. The existing black-and-white checkerboard-patterned floor would have daunted and limited many designers, but Taylor met the challenge of decorating the room with great aplomb. He used the tiled floor and pale-gray walls as an effective foil for the effervescent colors of a distinctive suite of eight Venetian chairs that he had bought from the estate of an Italian countess in Orbetello, Italy. The eighteenth-century chairs, with their intricately carved, green-rubbed wooden frames and steel-enforced splats, were upholstered alternately in solid shades of vibrant turquoise, green, yellow, purple, and raspberry silk. The chairs were placed in sets of four around a balanced pair of square brass folding card tables that came from Bergdorf-Goodman.

Lewis's card room also functioned as a garden room. The delicate fretwork cornice, which predated Taylor's decoration of the house, gave him the inspiration to screen the east window with whitewashed treillage. Exotic plants and towering palm trees also flourished in the card room, which, during the daytime, glowed with natural light that poured in through three successive pairs of French doors. The card room became one of Taylor's legendary interiors. It has been chronicled in the *New York Times Magazine* and twice in *House & Garden*. Sister Parish, the legendary interior decorator, visited the room when she was decorating a neighboring house during the 1970s. Reportedly, she was "horrified" when she saw the card room. She thought that it was too loud. When Parish's critique filtered back to Lewis and Taylor, they chuckled together in amusement. Both client and decorator were confident in their own tastes and in what they had created. Lewis has maintained the card room in its original state for more than forty years and has never considered changing it.

MR. AND MRS. DEWITT RUCKER

PEBBLE BEACH, CALIFORNIA, 1963

LIVING ROOM

Taylor infused a great deal of color into the Ruckers' Pebble Beach living room. He offset the predominantly white room with a Raimonds Staprans oil painting and luscious blueberry-blue and white fabric. Although the paisley-patterned print covered only the wing chair and several pillows, its vibrancy and boldness reverberated throughout the interior, validating one of Rudolph Schaeffer's key lessons. The mellow patina of the herringbone pine floor and the fruitwood of the seventeenth-century money-changer's table and the French provincial secretary also contributed richness and sophisticated rusticity to the room.

GARDEN ROOM

The blue-and-white color scheme characterized the garden room without being repetitive. Various textures, including the glazed ceramic tile floor, the love seat's "bumpy" cotton upholstery, and the tasseled handwoven wool window shades, were an effective foil to the solarium's principal source of color. The fauteuils' embroidered seat cushions and Helen Rucker's resourcefully arranged collection of Dutch delftware and Chinese export porcelains diffused the luxuriant shade of blue throughout the pristine interior.

MR. AND MRS. WILLIAM GREEN

SAN FRANCISCO, CALIFORNIA, 1964

DINING ROOM

Taylor outfitted the Greens' dining room in French provincial furniture—a throwback to one of Frances Elkins's favorite styles. He also maintained a background of white, which included the luxuriant soft glove leather that covered the dining chairs. The room's distinctive color scheme came from the collection of diverse blue-and-white early French, Portuguese, and Chinese export faïence accessorizing the breakfront, the dining table, and the shuttered wall. The antique lion, the lavabo, and the chandelier, all found by Taylor, were unique.

LIVING ROOM

Moroccan-inspired grille work instilled an exotic and light-filled backdrop in Bill and Frances Greens' Presidio Heights living room. The grouping of three tufted ottomans in the screened bay window created intimacy and coziness within the parameters of the large stately room. The tufted green seat cushions on the Italian-style black-framed open arm chairs and the pair of ottoman pillows maintained the color scheme from the adjacent entrance hall, which was carpeted in green-and-white wool.

MR. JAMES WILSON
MRS. ESTHER WILSON

NOGALES, ARIZONA, 1965

LIBRARY

In the library, plastered walls in a light terra cotta
and the aged patina of the parquet floor combined to create a monochromatic background
for an eclectic collection of antiques. An English
games table and a French Régence desk stood
in the forefront of the L-shaped room. The desk,
which was set into the bookcase-lined L,
balanced the games table and its four Régence
carved beechwood fauteuils. Chinese furnishings
in black lacquer and gilt contributed exoticism
to the classically decorated room. An Oriental
cabinet was placed against the south wall, midway into the room. The cabinet, which was
mounted to an ornately carved and gilded
wooden base, faced a six-panel embossed coromandel screen that stood, partially folded, next
to the desk.

The focal point of the library was the carved
amethyst marble Louis XV fireplace mantel. The
mantel anchored the library's seating area, which
was arranged at the far end of the room. Here, a
large sofa and three comparably scaled Louis XV
armchairs were underscored by an early
nineteenth-century Chinese silk carpet. The
luxurious narrow-wale and sculpted cinnamon
corduroy that covered the four pieces of furniture intensified the richness of the elegant
interior.

LIVING ROOM

At Wilson's request, the fifty-foot-long living room was furnished with several seating areas to accommodate large crowds as well as intimate get-togethers. The principal seating area, the focal point of the room, was anchored by a nineteen-foot-long banquette, custom-made to fill a deep alcove. An expansive and delicately worn antique net wall hanging adorned with floral re-embroidery in shades of royal blue and gold hung on the wall behind the sofa, complementing its plush Brunschwig & Fils Mozart velvet, also in royal blue. Sculpted Scalamandré velvet, in light indigo blue, covered a suite of French provincial-style armchairs grouped by Taylor in varied arrangements throughout the beamed and stone-floored great room. There were fourteen of these chairs, and their intricately carved and faintly antiqued gold-and-white wooden frames blended flawlessly with the diverse assortment of accompanying coffee and occasional tables abricated in stone, Byzantine mosaic, and gilded wood.

DINING ROOM

At the north end of the living room, a monumental pair of custom-carved ash double doors
opened into the dining room. The stone-floored
dining room, which stepped down a foot and
a half from the living room, was also impressive.
For the room, which measured forty-five feet in
length, Taylor and Wilson found in New York
a seventeenth-century English oak dining table
more than seventeen feet long, which accommodated a suite of two dozen Italian walnut
Baroque dining chairs as well as a pair of Louis
XVI walnut armchairs upholstered in black
leather. The tole twig chandelier, substantial
but delicate, that hung over the table infused
an organic element into the baronial decor.

POOL PAVILION

After the Wilson house was completed during the late 1960s, it wasn't long before Taylor persuaded Wilson that the compound needed a pool pavilion. The swimming pool that belonged to the original house still existed, and with Taylor's assurance that the pavilion would cost only thirty thousand dollars (it cost over ten times that amount), Wilson allowed him to proceed with the project. Porter and Steinwedell, following Taylor's instructions, drew the plans. They connected the two abutting buildings by incorporating a doorway that opened from the northeast corner of the dining room into an intimate L-shaped hallway. The hallway, which signaled the beginning of the pavilion, led to one of the two guest suites. It also doubled as the upper landing for the Herculean balustraded limestone staircase that descended over twenty feet to the pavilion floor. The lengthy descent not only created a twenty-foot-tall vaulted ceiling for the pavilion itself, but it also equalized the pavilion floor with the adjacent terrace that edged the swimming pool.

The pool pavilion was majestic, starting with its elaborate highly polished inlaid Venetian marble floor. The floor, with its principal ground of terra-cotta Rojoalcante, was dramatized by ornamental marquetry boldly patterned in Belgian black, Thassos white, and yellow sienna. Symmetry was also a key to the room design. A pair of oversized tufted banquettes and a pair of English-style club chairs, all upholstered in gold linen, framed the monumental carved limestone fireplace mantel. The mantel in turn was balanced by a pair of fifteen-foot-tall arched niches whose mirrored facades magnified the overall opulence of the room.

The pavilion abounded in antiques. Two matched French console tables, each one consisting of an off-white enameled top that was mounted to an ornate wrought-iron base, were semi-attached individually to the respective niches, complementing the Italian Baroque overmantel mirror, whose gold and gilt frame formed a scroll and plume design. On the western side of the pavilion, opposite the seating area, Taylor specified a pair of balancing games tables. The pedestal tables, with their slick black glass octagonal-shaped surfaces, offset an accompanying suite of eight antiqued black-and-gold Sheraton-style armchairs, the same chair that Taylor specified for the intimate pavilion dining room/games room.

Although the pavilion accommodated many guests, its principal function was to harmonize with the outdoors. Taylor merged the two environments effortlessly. He dominated the pavilion's western elevation with three successive pairs of full-length glazed double doors. Each pair of doors was recessed into a limestone-trimmed archway and completely screened by Moroccan-inspired grille work. The intricately pierced wooden grilles, which were also inset into the archways, contained tall divisions of hinged panels that opened, in conjunction with the double doors, onto the poolside terrace.

Contrary to Taylor's initial assurance, the original swimming pool had to be enlarged, lengthwise and widthwise, in order to be centered on the pavilion and the double flight of cascading steps that ascended to the rear courtyard. The stone courtyard was expansive. It continued the elaborate sequence of balustraded promenades and fountain-laden courtyards that terraced down from the main house to the eleventh, and lowest, level of the compound, where the tennis court, spectator's pavilion, rose garden, and wisteria arbor were sited.

MR. AND MRS. WILLIAM E. ROBERTS

WOODSIDE, CALIFORNIA, 1965

When Bill and Gerry Roberts commissioned Taylor to decorate their Woodside house, they expected to raze the Tudor-style manse because it contained a warren of small rooms. The Robertses, who were seasoned travelers, wanted the decor to reflect the localities of their worldly sojourns. They also asked for interiors "that a horse would feel comfortable in." Taylor assured his clients that he could meet their explicit desires within the framework of the existing building.

LIVING ROOM

Taylor furnished the Robertses' living room eclectically within hardy and rugged surroundings. He exposed the ceiling's rough-hewn beams and added vertical spans of the strapping supports, intermittently, along the perimeter of the room. Dark brown stain coated the beams and all the woodwork that bordered the stone-walled room.

The living room's principal banquette nestled in the curvature of the windowed wall overlooking the Robertses' bucolic property. Taylor upholstered the commodious seating in soft-ribbed velvet, whose rich hue of chocolate brown corresponded with the stain of the wood. He also placed a shaggy Greek goat's-wool rug on the floor in response to another wish of his clients. They requested that the anthracite shag rug be impermeable to cigarette ashes.

Diverse textures and boldly graphic patterns complemented the Robertses' living room. A pair of old Mexican stone capitals served as the coffee tables alongside the low banquette, and authentic zebra skin covered the set of diminutive frog chairs. The fanciful Baroque scroll sconce that projected from the wall further exemplified Taylor's singular and resourceful taste.

DINING ROOM

England, which was one of the Robertses' favorite destinations, inspired Taylor's plan for their dining room. The success of the interior also depended on his ability to miraculously transform its original "nondescript boxlike" blueprint.

Taylor solved the problem by heightening the dining room. He created a peaked and beamed ceiling within the parameters of the crawl space that lay empty above the banal interior. The beams both fortified the dining room and created consistency with the design of the adjacent living room.

The Robertses' dining room was distinguished by vibrant red burlap covering its walls and ceiling. The textured material, which was also used for the window curtains, brightened the interior and contrasted effectively with the old dining table, the Jacobean chairs, the Gothic fireplace, and the Mexican tin chandelier.

House & Garden featured the Roberts house twice in 1966. On the day that Fred Lyon photographed the house for the magazine, Taylor was in his usual form. He arrived late for the photo shoot and immediately began directing everything that was going on. Taylor, who thought no one took a good photograph of his work unless he was overseeing the shoot, did his best work in front of the camera. He often finished decorating a room while the photographs were being taken. Even when Lyon was breaking down his equipment, with Taylor there was usually another shot to be taken. Taylor always prevailed. His great ideas during the Roberts photo shoot, along with Lyon's well-composed photographs, generated a twelve-page article as well as a cover for the magazine.

MR. AND MRS. STANLEY BEYER

BEL AIR, CALIFORNIA, 1966

S tanley and Lynn Beyer's initial meeting with Taylor in 1966 galva-
nized their long-standing and mutually respected relationship with
him, in spite of the fact that he was slightly arrogant at first. After Taylor looked around the Beyers' house, he asked them how long they
had been married. When they answered him, he quipped back to
them "In ten years, you've never bought a good piece of furniture?"
Fortunately, the Beyers were game for Taylor's candor, guidance, and
connoisseurship in choosing the appropriate antiques for their English-style whitewashed brick house.

Within a short period of time after the meeting, Taylor and Stanley Beyer traveled together for ten days throughout Europe where they
assembled over one hundred pieces of furniture and objets d'art for the
house. Their thorough and inspiring visits to most of the notable antiques shops and private dealers in London bore a compilation of pedigreed tables, chairs, desks, secretaries, and breakfronts. The extensive
selection of chairs included one dozen Chippendale dining chairs that
Taylor told Beyer "were worthwhile and he had to have them," despite
the fact that dining chairs were already being custom-made for the
house. Taylor felt so strongly about the Chippendale chairs that he
told his client that he would "get rid of the other chairs."

LIVING ROOM BY FIREPLACE

White Brunschwig & Fils Athos chintz,
decorated in mint-green foliage, created the
refreshing gardenlike backdrop for the Beyers'
living room. Taylor anchored the spacious interior with a pair of custom Moroccan-style white
wool shag rugs that were subtly patterned in a
black diamond design. The unequally sized rugs
underscored three distinct seating areas.

Taylor's arrangement of the furniture alongside the living room's fireplace created intimacy
within the spacious interior. The plan included
a love seat, a gilded Italian open armchair, and
a pair of antique Queen Anne wing chairs.
The chairs, with their textured white and beige
fabrics and exquisite fringed trim, were almost
translucent. This quality enabled the grouping's
antique tables and accessories, and the love seat's
quilted white-and-green chintz, to express an
unrestrained composure.

LIVING ROOM

The quilted Brunschwig & Fils chintz, one of Taylor's favorite patterns, was paramount to the seating area that balanced the fireplace grouping on the opposite side of the living room. Here, Taylor arranged a commodious sofa and three English-style club chairs around one of the coffee tables purchased in London. The antique table, with its lacquered Chinese gold-and-black decorated top, glistened. Its elegance and distinction were commensurate with the book-lined antique chinoiserie secretary and the antique lacquer and mother-of-pearl burgauté chest that sat alongside one of the club chairs. The brilliant green glaze of the old Oriental pottery conical bowl accessorizing the coffee table also enriched the setting's luxuriant hue.

LIVING ROOM

Taylor's skilled arrangement of antiques in the Beyers' living room created balance between casualness and formality. Although every antique in the room was a major piece, their importance was tempered by the interior's airy and restful palette. Taylor could not have composed a more beautiful living room for the Beyers, even if he had set it in an authentic English garden. Lynn Beyer loved the "Enchanted Cottage" look.

Taylor's "on-target" interpretation of her penchant also carried over to her and her husband's next house. When the Beyers built their Holmby Hills house in 1975, they blueprinted a living room that replicated the first one. Although the new living room was slightly improved in terms of space, the Beyers just moved all their furniture into the new interior.

MASTER BEDROOM AND SITTING ROOM

White chintz, with its bird and rose and green flower print, created a cheerful gardenlike setting in the Beyers' bedroom suite. The suite, which consisted of an intimate sleeping alcove and a spacious sitting area, was light and airy. In the alcove, Taylor covered the walls and the ceiling with a multicolored cotton print turned sideways in order to enhance its application. He also quilted the fabric, using the textured material for the antique French headboard, pillows, bedspread, and upholstered pieces. Taylor amplified the openness of the master bedroom suite by removing the original ceiling in the sitting area. The newly heightened ceiling, with its planked fabrication and exposed beams, contributed subtle rusticity to the setting. It also complemented the division's collection of eclectic furnishings. They included an old country French secretary, a gilded Georgian walnut mirror, and a suite of lustrous Japanese red-lacquered coffee tables. Giacometti and Elkins were also incorporated into the design. The loop secretary chair and the variety of plaster lamps arranged throughout the suite were throwbacks to the two avant-garde designers.

ENTRANCE HALL TOWARD DINING ROOM

The Beyers' entrance hall was paved in Taylor's favored windowpane pattern. The baronial floor, with its white oak wood–bordered inserts of polished white marble, underscored an antique chinoiserie decorated English table. Although the table was late eighteenth century, its distinguished provenance did not dissuade Taylor from accessorizing it with a Giacometti-style cup-and-ball plaster vase and an abstract brass sculpture.

The entrance hall proffered an absorbing view into the dining room, where Taylor's choice of color and texture was flawless. The room's faux-painted pine walls, off-white custom wool rug, and apricot velvet upholstery harmonized with the late eighteenth-century English dining table, the suite of Chippendale chairs, and the Baccarat candelabra accessorizing the table.

DAUGHTER'S BEDROOM

The Beyers' daughter's bedroom was enchanting
and picturesque with its overall application of
blue-and-white Toile de Jouy. A Delft-blue
broadloom area rug fringed in chenille underscored the three-quarter-size canopy bed and the
pair of Syrie Maugham tufted armchairs.

The canopy bed was especially beautiful.
Taylor trimmed it in scalloped looped linen.
He also underlined its curtains in blue-and-
white checked cotton, infusing a subtle contrast
into the bedroom's decor.

Distinctive accessories placed the finishing
touches on the bedroom. The French gray stone
mantel, with its large carved seashell motif and
herringbone-patterned interior, displayed a di-
versity of blue-and-white delftware. The Dutch
porcelain, which was ideal for the bedroom,
was enhanced by its backdrop—an old mirror
decoratively framed in real shells.

The toile bedroom was replicated as the guest
room in the Beyers' present house. The great
effort expended in re-creating the bedroom three
decades later is clearly a tribute to Taylor and his
"fabulous taste." Stanley and Lynn Beyer have
always felt that "Michael was sensational!"

MR. AND MRS. CHARLES W. FAY JR.

SAN FRANCISCO, CALIFORNIA, 1966

Charles and Dorothy Fay lived at 1055 California Street on Nob Hill. Lewis Parsons Hobart (1873–1954) designed the revered 1920s Beaux-Arts apartment building that stood across the street from Grace Cathedral. Taylor had already worked for the Fays at their previous homes in San Francisco and Woodside.

Taylor unified the interiors of the Fays' apartment by painting its walls soft gray. The monochromatic backdrop complemented their collection of family heirlooms as well as the pieces that Taylor selected for the apartment.

LIVING ROOM BY TAPESTRY

In the living room, a Persian carpet served as the foundation for Taylor's arrangement of seating. He placed one of the principal sofas before an eighteenth-century Flemish tapestry depicting a forest scene with birdlife. This splendid antique textile figured prominently in the interior without intrusion from the museum-quality pieces that surrounded it.

Luxurious fabrics in neutral tones covered the upholstered pieces and harmonized with the decor's antique furnishings. Silk velvet corduroy in chocolate brown covered the pair of large sofas, an armchair, and the room's full-length tieback curtains. The frog chairs, which the Fays purchased from the Robertses when they moved from their Woodside home, were equally suitable in the Nob Hill living room.

LIVING ROOM TOWARD DINING ROOM AND LIBRARY

The living room opened through a pair of double doors into the combination dining room and library. The entryway, which was crowned by a panel, ornamentally decorated in plaster relief, offset the living room's L-shaped seating area and French provincial writing table. The plaster Giacometti-style desk lamp and the Robert Rauschenberg lithograph hanging above the desk gave a contemporary accent to the traditional salon.

LIVING ROOM BY FIREPLACE

Taylor created an L-shaped seating area by the fireplace. He united a pair of armless sofas into a corner banquette. Honey-colored velvet covered the seating which was skirted in bouillon cord fringe. The pair of Louis XVI fauteuils and the mother-of-pearl coffee table from India completed the intimate vignette.

DINING ROOM AND LIBRARY

The dining table, with its gilded dolphin legs and continental dining chairs, was set amid a backdrop of bookcase-lined walls and a pair of full-length windows overlooking the city. Although the windows were curtained in chocolate-brown silk velvet corduroy and the chair seats were covered in dark brown leather, Taylor opted for a multicolored savonnerie carpet. The French carpet was composed of muted shades, including salmon, gray, beige, and green. The porcelain tureen on the table was Chinese export.

The oil painting by Roland Peterson, the Bay Area artist, contributed vibrant color and abstract composition to the seating area nestled between an early nineteenth-century coromandel screen and a built-in bookcase. Equally complimentary to the vignette was the velvet upholstery. The luxurious fabric evoked unbridled comfort and also perpetuated constancy within the apartment.

MRS. DIANA DOLLAR HICKINGBOTHAM

ENTRANCE HALL

The largest interior in Hickingbotham's thirteen-room house was the main entrance hall. The marble-floored hall, which set the tone for the house's elegantly appointed rooms, was sparsely furnished. A suite of four antique-white Louis XVI chairs, a pair of French Empire ormolu bouillotte tables, and a pair of eighteenth-century Italian marble-topped pier tables were all that Taylor specified for the room. His astute selection and strategic placement of the furniture in the hall enabled it to be converted readily into an imposing space for large cocktail and dinner parties as well as dancing.

LIVING ROOM

Taylor furnished Hickingbotham's living room and dining room with similar restraint. In the living room, an eighteenth-century Samarkand carpet shaded in muted earth tones offset the principal arrangement of furniture—a settee and a suite of six overscaled French chairs. Sculpted Scalamandré pale-green velvet, which covered each of these pieces, was also specified for the sumptuous full-length tieback curtains. A large painted paper Chinese screen, a pair of antique rock-crystal chandeliers, and Hickingbotham's collection of Chinese jade augmented the rare beauty of this petite salon.

DINING ROOM

The dining room was an amalgam of French and English antiques, all underscored by a bare floor of new parquet made from various hardwoods. Although the room was washed predominantly in off-white, Taylor interjected restrained touches of pale and medium blue into the decor. He accessorized the dining room with Hickingbotham's collection of fine Chinese and Danish porcelains. The Louis XVI cane-backed dining chairs were upholstered in a blue-and-white Bargello. The off-white tieback curtains were edged in a swathe of blue velvet.

LIBRARY TOWARD BAY WINDOW

The incorporation of a new bay window into Hickingbotham's library expanded the room and allowed for the installation of her Louis XV-style bureau plat. Tieback curtains in striped ombré silk from Old World Weavers contributed subtle colors of green, raspberry, and blue to the setting. The collection of fine antiques in the library also included an eighteenth-century Chinese coromandel screen in rust.

LIBRARY TOWARD FIREPLACE

Taylor created a cozy sitting area by the library's antique marble fireplace with a grouping of French bergeres. The nineteenth-century overstuffed pine chair and ottoman, with its luxurious cut-velvet upholstery from Scalamandré, demonstrated the designer's attention to both scale and comfort. The library's bare floor was of new parquet made from various hardwoods.

MR. AND MRS. CHARLES W. FAY JR.

APTOS BEACH, CALIFORNIA, 1967

Charles and Dorothy Fay commissioned Taylor, just on the heals of finishing their city apartment, to decorate their vacation house in Aptos Beach, California, sixty five miles south of San Francisco. Once again, Taylor collaborated with Porter and Steinwedell on the project: a gable-roofed wood-frame and stucco house.

The Fays' experienced design team created a beachside house in which casualness and spontaneity were de rigueur. The retreat welcomed family and friends alike. There was plenty of room for entertaining, and overnight company was easily accommodated in the three first-floor guestrooms.

LIVING ROOM AND DINING ROOM

Porter and Steinwedell designed the living room and dining room in combination with each other. Both rooms shared a heightened pitched ceiling that was beamed and inventively lined with woven willow. The plant-filled living room was adroitly furnished with two seating areas. The principal grouping was established by a large sofa covered in white cotton duck and accented with solid royal blue and navy blue and white Mexican pillows. It sat against the living room's main wall, facing the fireplace on the opposite side of the room. A pair of equipales chairs and end tables, with sprayed white frames, were also incorporated into the arrangement.

A love seat, replicating the design of the sofa and identically upholstered, sat perpendicular to the fireplace wall. Its placement marked the entrance to the dining room, which formed an L at the fore of the house.

Taylor decorated the dining room amid the inviting backdrop of book-lined shelves. This ingenious idea, conveyed from the Fays' San Francisco apartment, was equally appealing at their beach house. Space was at a premium in the house, and the library wall in the dining room addressed that issue. The dining table and its *equipales* chairs awaited the voracious reader as well as the ravenous gourmet. Charles and Dorothy Fay welcomed both into their home.

BEACHSIDE DECK

The living room opened onto a spacious beach-side deck spanning the entire width of the house. Porter and Steinwedell edged the wooden deck with wide railings that doubled as bench seating. They also included a simple staircase that stepped down from the deck to the beach.

Entertaining al fresco was a way of life for the Fays. Their deck was dotted with *equipales* seating, plenty of potted plants, and two verdant shade trees that grew up through the decking. It also had a built-in dining table. Taylor, who always integrated nature into his plans, didn't have to go far to find the right prop when he designed the dining area. He adopted the tree that stood closest to the house, allowing it to become part of the vignette.

Taylor designed the dining table around the tree. His fusion of the two components was ingenious. He left a hole in the center of the round table in order to accommodate the tree. According to Fred Lyon, "Dorothy Fay pain-stakingly trained that tiny sapling until it grew through the opening to shade the table." As the tree matured, the dining table became an exotic oasis with its rush matting and permanent umbrella of flourishing foliage.

MR. AND MRS. ROBERT FOLGER MILLER JR.

HILLSBOROUGH, CALIFORNIA, 1968

LIVING ROOM

Bob and Maryon Miller's living room, although
spacious, challenged them and Taylor. Their
mutual goal was to create warmth and coziness
in the twenty-foot-by-forty-foot room.
Fortunately, the Millers had already purchased
a collection of museum-quality furniture at Celia
Clark's auction. They also were antiquarians
themselves.

Trompe l'oeil marked the successful decor in
the living room. The walls and ceiling beams
were painted to resemble pine paneling. The
parchment glazing, elegant and restful, was
commensurate with the Millers' furnishings
and Taylor's proposed design for the room.

Three muted Bessarabian carpets floating on
the living room's richly stained oak floor also enhanced the interior's classic timelessness. One
of the carpets, which aligned with the fireplace,
established the room's three divisions of seating.

Taylor arranged two of the seating areas
alongside opposite edges of the carpet, facing
each other. Set perpendicular to the fireplace,
each vignette was composed of a sofa, a bronze
and tortoiseshell–top low table, and a Queen
Anne armchair. Luxurious velvet and damask
in neutral shades covered the sofas and chairs.

The juxtaposition of contemporary art with
eclectic furnishings added interest to the living
room. The oil painting hanging above the mantel was by Robert Guerrier, the French Modernist, and one of the flanking console tables
was Venetian. Taylor had the matching table
made by a local craftsman. He also divided the
Millers' twelve-panel coromandel screen in half,
placing it in equal sections on opposite sides of
the room.

Bob and Maryon Miller's living room was one
of Taylor's legendary interiors. The room was
featured prominently in several magazines and
newspapers, including *House & Garden* and
Town and Country.

MR. AND MRS. JOHN C. WALKER

SAN FRANCISCO, CALIFORNIA, 1970

The five-story wood-shake townhouse that John (Sandy) Walker designed on a verdant site in Pacific Heights was "like living in a treehouse." Walker nestled the house creatively on the sloping piece of property overlooking San Francisco Bay.

The decorating of the house is a humorous story unto itself. When the building's construction was completed during the late 1960s, Taylor promised Walker that he would furnish it—momentarily—for a *House & Garden* feature. Dorothea Walker, the *House & Garden* correspondent and Walker's long-standing friend, supervised the assignment for the magazine.

On the appointed morning of the photo shoot, Walker arrived at the house with Fred Lyon, who was going to take the photographs. She and Lyon discovered that the interiors were completely empty except for a white sofa in the living room and a brass canopy bed in the upstairs master bedroom. Walker and Lyon were somewhat bewildered, but just for a moment. They both knew only too well that such conduct was not out of character for Taylor. Fortunately, he appeared at the house with a large van full of furniture and his crew of helpers, ten minutes after their arrival. Taylor, always resourceful, had borrowed the furniture from his own house.

The crew unloaded the van, stacking all the furniture, accessories, and giant plants in the Walkers' motor court. They then began moving the vast assemblage in and out of the house until Taylor was satisfied with the arrangement. Per usual for Taylor, it was not a fast process. Lyon was finally sanctioned to begin photographing the house by noon on the following day.

LIVING ROOM

Sandy and Pat Walker's sixteen-foot-tall beamed living room occupied the top two levels of the house. The weighty beams were over one hundred years old. They came from a demolished bridge that once led from Mill Valley, California, into Sausalito, above Richardson Bay. The old supports buttressed the room's sizable skylight that Walker set at the height of twenty-two feet. Its addition of airiness and natural light into the house appealed to Taylor's design aesthetic.

The living room's floor-to-ceiling windows welcomed additional light into the interior, especially the pair that balanced the room's north wall and projected out toward the Bay. The backdrop of white walls was also a natural canvas for Taylor's adroit staging.

Taylor decorated the living room with his signature look. He slipcovered the sofa in white cotton and added a mixture of wicker armchairs, baskets, and Mexican tin trays from Cost Plus to the venue. He also included his infamous antler chair. The requisite arrangements of towering Ficus Benjamina trees in the room branded the design a "Michael Taylor" original.

LIVING ROOM TOWARD FIREPLACE

The horde of inventory in the van included several enormous contemporary paintings that were rented from the Nicholas Wilder Gallery in Los Angeles. Taylor often called art dealers on the spur of the moment in San Francisco, persuading them to lend a painting or two for a photo shoot. He usually sent his crew to the intended gallery to retrieve the work just as he was calling the dealer. In this case, because Wilder's gallery was located in Los Angeles, Taylor planned ahead. He borrowed several oils, including a vibrant Kenneth Noland stripe painting that Walker installed above the living room mantel.

DINING ROOM

Helen Frankenthaler's powerful oil painting, also from Wilder's gallery, dominated the Walkers' dining room, which was situated ten steps below the living room. The painting's vibrant poured colors of yellow, purple, coral, and green emanated throughout the white interior.

Taylor furnished the dining room simply, allowing Walker's architecture to lead. He opted for French country pieces in the room. They included caned Louis XVI dining chairs and a handpainted cabinet that sat to the left of the staircase. But most important to Taylor's design was the dining room's relationship with nature. The room's unadorned full-length wall of glass opened onto the house's front terrace, perpetuating the combined indoor-outdoor ambience.

MR. AND MRS. STANLEY BEYER

MALIBU, CALIFORNIA, 1971

ENTRANCE HALL

A concave wall of glass maintained the semblance between the house's rock-garden courtyard and its entrance hall, where islands of Yosemite slate—surrounded by mortar and concrete—established the innovative free-form flooring used throughout the interior. Walls of board-formed concrete and granite boulders perpetuated Lautner and Taylor's narrow focus on organic appointments for the house, including an overpowering twenty-one-ton boulder (the largest in the house) that offset the steps leading down from the entrance hall into the living room.

LIVING ROOM

In the Beyers' vast sunken living room, three
forty-two-inch-deep sofas were cast into the
concrete of the building in advance of its
construction, generating a curvilinear foundation for three distinct sitting areas and Taylor's
requisite overstuffed white Crowder chenille
cushions and ball pillows. Yosemite slate,
overscaled boulders and chisel-sided black
granite tables melded flawlessly with the house's
all-encompassing integration with the Pacific
Ocean. Lynn Beyer marveled at the house.
She said it was like living inside of a piece of
modern sculpture.

STUDY AND DINING AREA

Taylor's design for the study and dining area, which stepped up from the main floor, was consistent with the living room. The study's sofa sat in balance to the round granite dining table and the Greek klismos-style dining chairs. The openness of the house's floor plan, in conjunction with the property's panoramic setting, created an expansive sensibility for the Beyers.

MR. AND MRS. JOHN G. BOWES

SAN FRANCISCO, CALIFORNIA, 1971

Taylor's first commission for John and Frances Bowes was the interior decoration of their brown shingled Arts and Crafts–style house in Pacific Heights, designed by Bernard Maybeck (1862–1957), the renowned Bay area architect. The Boweses were seasoned collectors of contemporary art, and Taylor created interiors that complemented their collection as well as the vernacular of Maybeck's architecture.

LIVING ROOM

When the Boweses purchased the house, its redwood-paneled walls and ceiling beams were already bleached. Fortunately, the neutral palette facilitated Taylor's plan for the interiors. He covered the living room's fifteen-foot tufted sofa and English-style armchairs in white Crowder chenille. He also skirted them copiously in bouillon cord fringe.

The enormity of the living room pieces related in scale to the room's focal point; the baronial stone fireplace. The floor-to-ceiling hearth was imposing and its medieval overtones sharpened the modernity of the furniture, paintings, and sculpture. Its hardy patina also correlated with the pair of low stone coffee tables that fronted the sofa.

DINING ROOM

The Boweses often entertained at home, hosting family and friends alike. One evening, both of their mothers, Dorothy Fay and Ruth Bowes, were the guests. All was well until dinner was announced. The two septuagenarians, who were comfortably seated on the living room sofa during cocktails, were unable to free themselves without rescue from the clutches of Taylor's deep tufted model.

Princess Margaret was the guest of honor at another one of the Boweses' seated dinner parties. The eight dinner guests included Taylor. He was working on the Boweses' new dining room at the time. Ironically, because ground had just been broken for the addition, the Boweses' guests were treated to a view of the huge empty pit in the garden through the existing dining room's leaded glass windows.

The new dining room blended flawlessly with the original house. Taylor, collaborating with Porter and Steinwedell, infused Maybeck characteristics into the addition. They replicated the bleached paneling and ceiling beams as well as the leaded glass doors and windows. Taylor also furnished the room cleanly with a round wooden pedestal table and wicker barrel chairs.
John and Frances Bowes valued Taylor. They, like many of his other clients, thought he was exorbitant. Taylor liked to call Frances to say he was on his way over to the house. He usually wanted to go over one of his bills for their job with her and John. Frances always told Taylor that John was not at home. Taylor knew better, retorting to Frances, "Oh yes he is. He's locked himself in the bathroom. He wants to avoid discussing my bill!" Although Taylor was right, he and the Boweses enjoyed a meaningful professional and social relationship throughout his career. Frances recalled, "Taylor made everything so much fun." She and her husband also realized, looking back in time, that Taylor was not expensive. He guided his clients, enhancing the value of their homes through the improvements he made. Taylor also advised his clients to purchase art and antiques that appreciated substantially in value.

MR. AND MRS. WILLIAM H. HAMM III

SAN FRANCISCO, CALIFORNIA, 1972

When William and Candy Hamm hired Taylor to extensively re-model and decorate their Presidio Heights townhouse in 1972, he was their seventh interior designer. Candy, who is extremely knowl-edgeable about design and the decorative arts, found that she was mentoring her designers not the other way around. Fortunately, that bothersome exercise ceased with Taylor, who was "going to tell me [Candy] what to do." He introduced Candy and Bill to worldwide sources that purveyed a compilation of rare antiques for their French Normandy-style townhouse.

The remodeling of the Hamms' townhouse, which took six years to execute, included enclosing its new plaster, flagstone, and brass-bordered entrance forecourt with a glass skylight. Four Versailles planters, profusely filled with specimen white camellia trees brought from North Carolina to San Francisco, stood as sentries inside the fore-court, framing, in pairs, its street-side entrance and the front door leading into the townhouse's entrance hall.

ENTRANCE HALL

A commanding Régence commode, accessorized with a lotus bowl in Blanc de Chine, and a gilt-framed Régence mirror, itself mounted onto a mirrored wall, foreshadowed the exemplary antiques outfitting the interiors of the Hamms' townhouse. The entrance hall, which was paved in bleached oak patterned in a basket weave, was located on the townhouse's piano nobile along with its principal rooms.

LIVING ROOM TOWARD SCREEN

Taylor created a welcoming palette in the Hamms' living room. He—by design—outfitted the salon with fabrics and textiles that had a three-dimensional quality. Subtly textured fabrics in cream silk, chenille, and embroidery covered the walls and the upholstered pieces, dressing down the impact of the room's rare antiques, including its coffee table, which was a fifteenth-century Byzantine tomb door mounted on a Taylor signature stone capital. The sisal rug, conceived and custom designed by Candy Hamm and Robert Walker—the renowned trompe l'oeil artist from London who was a pioneer in painting sisal—contributed both sophistication and informality to the cozy room that "invited one in to curl up and read a book."

The pièce de résistance in the living room was the extraordinary twelve-panel K'ang-shi screen. The screen, one of only twenty-six screens of its type in the world (ten of the screens survive today) once stood in the Imperial Palace in China and was given by the empress to a French family in anticipation of the Boxer Rebellion. The empress wanted to protect the screen from destruction. The screen was eventually acquired by C. T. Loo, the definitive Oriental art dealer, who in turn sold it to the Hamms. Their acquisition of the screen, which was somewhat involved, constitutes an amusing story.

Taylor and C. T. Loo knew each other quite well. Taylor frequently visited Loo at his shop in Paris. When Loo telephoned Taylor in San Francisco to tell him about the screen he had acquired, Taylor put a hold on it—sight unseen—for the Hamms. Loo immediately sent Taylor a color transparency of the screen, which he showed to his clients. The Hamms recognized the screen's rarity and purchased it immediately. They also respected Taylor's unerring eye for quality and his compelling endorsement of the antiquity.

Loo shipped the screen—under guard—to San Francisco—in twelve individual crates lined in velvet. Elwells, along with the security detail, then brought the shipment from the holding cages at customs, where it had also remained under guard, to the Hamms' house. Conservators from the de Young Museum's Oriental art department unpacked each crate with kid gloves, slowly and laboriously cleaning with tightly wound Q-tips the residue of opium dust and tobacco smoke from each panel. Amazingly, the conservators recognized the screen as they studied it. The screen was the centerfold in the book on Loo's venerable collection that was for sale at the museum. Taylor brought the book to his clients, who were extremely pleased to see their screen prominently displayed and documented in the monograph.

Unfortunately, when the screen was finally assembled (in the Hamms' forecourt), "a catastrophe ensued" because it was too tall for the living room. Taylor never asked Loo for the height of the screen, and the townhouse's previous architect had lowered the living room ceiling.

Taylor, who "always landed on his feet," offered the perfect solution. He merely moved the living room sofa three feet away from the wall, had Porter and Steinwedell (they were designing the Hamms' dining room at the time) design a six-inch-deep trench to be dug into the new oak floor behind the sofa, and installed the screen in place, allowing it to skim just under the top of the room's ceiling.

LIVING ROOM CLOSEUP

Candy Hamm, accompanied by Taylor, purchased at auction a pair of gilt-bronze-mounted
rock-crystal lamps for her living room side tables.
The Louis XV–style lamps, each with five
cushion-cut rock-crystal specimens and rocaille
gilt-bronze bases, came from the Duchess of
Windsor's Bois de Boulogne villa in Paris. The
lamps' warm cream silk shades lined in peach
silk and interlined with pink Chinese silk, in
combination with their distinctive amber-colored
lightbulbs, cast an iridescent glow, highlighting
the living room's embroidery-draped side table
and its balancing gilt Régence table and warm
brown Brescia marble top. The Chinese frog
cachepots, lined in copper, came from the
collection of Pauline de Rothschild—the fashion
icon and tastemaker.

LIVING ROOM BY WINDOWS

Billowing curtains of warm cream Brunschwig &
Fils silk taffeta created a luxurious backdrop for
an eclectic grouping of furniture, which included
a Korean tea table inlaid with mother-of-pearl
and a cane-backed gesso French desk chair that
contained its original leather seat cushion. The
sisal rug's hand-painted Greek key design in
deep bronze and white, the faux-Brescia marble
baseboard also painted by Walker, and the
crown moldings' warm yellow gold fillet added
dimension to the setting.

LIVING ROOM TOWARD FIREPLACE

The Régence Brescia marble fireplace mantel and its offsetting pair of eighteenth-century rouge-Languedoc marble-topped Roman rococo gilt-wood consoles were also pivotal to the living room. The biscuit-colored brown mantel, which Taylor and Hamm located during one of their many trips to Paris, underscored an imposing gilt mirror—also from the Régence period. The fifteenth-century gilt candelabra displayed on the mantel were carved by Effingham the Elder, the preeminent English wood carver of the seventeenth century. Taylor's selection of straw baskets for the intimate setting was one of passionate scrutiny.

DINING ROOM

Taylor, in collaboration with Porter and Stein-wedell, remodeled the Hamms' dining room into a cushion-cut diamond-shaped interior that was a compendium of Andes black Brazilian granite, mirrored walls, and sophisticated recessed cove lighting composed of lightbulbs specially chosen for their wattage and glow. The Hamms' dining room, which took two years to complete, was one of the most opulent rooms ever created by Taylor (the room resembled a large Fabergé box). He traveled to the quarry in South America personally to select the granite that paved the dining room floor and formulated the room's substantial baseboard, specially carved Bombay double-ogee-edged crown molding, and table top.

The single piece of black granite that was used for the dining table took one year to locate and carve in Brazil. The table top, which followed the shape of the dining room, was scored six inches from its triple-ogee-edged border and weighed one ton. The table and its steel-reinforced stone pedestals, along with the accompanying floor (which was scored to resemble huge diamonds), baseboards, and moldings required a closely engineered infrastructure of steel pillars and ties underneath the poured-concrete dining room floor, which completely withstood, along with the china and crystal, San Francisco's Loma Prieta earthquake. (The Hamms were hosting a dinner party for twenty guests during the 1989 earthquake.)

However, long before the table top endured the devastating earthquake, it was dredged from the harbor after the freighter carrying it from Brazil, through the Panama Canal, sank upon arriving at its intended destination of Long Beach, California. Candy, learning about the catastrophe, hoped that the table top would not be recovered. She (unlike Taylor) was concerned about its rigorous weight and would have preferred to have a much lighter table in her dining room.

Candy was especially pleased with the dining room's console table, which was another superb find on one of her European sojourns with Taylor. The table was English—of the William Kent school (Kent was the preeminent English architect, landscape architect, and furniture designer during the eighteenth century). It was distinguished by an imposing and intricately carved (in the round) and gilded swan that glided gracefully through a swamp of carved and gilded cattail reeds.

DINING ROOM CLOSE-UP

Candy Hamm accessorized her dining table exquisitely. A collection of rock crystal, which included orbs, obelisks, and Chinese chops purchased in Paris, glistened against the backdrop of the black granite. The candlelit crystal chandelier from St. Petersburg, which hung from the dining room's domed plaster ceiling, complemented the black-lacquered Oriental chest and its carved and gilded wooden stand that Taylor sold to the Hamms. Candy had long admired the antique chest that once stood in Taylor's entrance hall at Sea Cliff. Candy Hamm thinks about Taylor regularly and remembers him telling her, "Every morning when you wake up, I want you to thank me for the furniture, objects, and porcelains you bought in London and Paris. It really isn't out there any more."

GARDEN ROOM

The Hamms' hexagonal garden room, with its trellised interior, domed trompe l'oeil ceiling painted by Robert Walker, and engaging views of the garden, was enchanting. Taylor found the hexagonal limestone table on the Left Bank in Paris. He also outfitted the room with a suite of one of his favorite chairs—the matchstick chair. Taylor copied the armchair from the model originally designed by Syrie Maugham. The chair, with its sawtooth frieze and inlaid matchstick marquetry, was distinctive. Taylor enjoyed the garden room as much as the Hamms. He loved to sit facing the garden, gazing at the topiary reindeer created by Bob Bell, and eat charlotte mousse specially prepared for him by the Hamms' cook every time he visited them.

MR. AND MRS. WARREN H. CLARK
SAN FRANCISCO, CALIFORNIA, 1973

LIVING ROOM

Taylor, like Elsie de Wolfe (1865–1950) before him, eschewed the darkness and heaviness of Victoriana when he decorated Warren and Monica Clark's Victorian townhouse. He freshened and reinterpreted the historic style with vibrant color and varied intensities of pattern.

In the living room, the walls were covered in a restful garden scene with flora and fauna painstakingly hand-painted on bare sheets of wallpaper by Garth Benton, the prominent West Coast muralist. Benton was inspired by several sheets of eighteenth-century Chinese wallpaper that Taylor owned and wanted to expand upon for the Clark commission. Its engaging colors—including pink, raspberry, purple, and varied shades of green—echoed throughout the verdant interior.

The living room's principal sofa was upholstered in deep green tufted moiré. It was skirted in white bouillon cord fringe, imparting additional detail and distinction to the handsomely fabricated piece of furniture that purportedly once belonged to Greta Garbo.

The Clarks' Victorian living room embraced an eclectic range of furniture unusual for the era. The stacked chinoiserie-style low tables, the Sheraton side chair, and the Louis XVI bergère would not have appeared in the historic interior. The striped silk taffeta tablecloth, the slipcovered cabbage rose chintz, and the textured golden straw rug were also revolutionary departures.

LIVING ROOM BAY

Taylor's plan for the living room capitalized on its intimate bay window. He recessed a love seat into the shuttered niche, expanding the para-meters of the "prettiest Victorian room ever seen" by Mark Hampton (1940–1998), the legendary interior decorator. The small sofa, which updated the Victorian prototype, was uphol-stered in a pale lime-yellow silk and adorned with one large tassel on each of its arm fronts. Taylor found the distinctive pair of Venetian blackamoor jardinières in a London antiques shop.

The Syrie Maugham armchairs balancing the love seat and the Victorian Chinese lacquer tea table contributed to the living room's successful design. They too were simplified renditions of Victorian models, and their tufted upholstery of dark-brown cotton velvet tempered the room's color scheme. The diminutive gilded stool was purchased by Taylor in London.

MR. AND MRS. GEORGE R. McKEON

HILLSBOROUGH, CALIFORNIA, 1973

While George and Elaine McKeon were building their stone and half-timbered English-style house in Hillsborough, California, during the early 1970s, their architect, Angus MacSweeny, died midway through the project. John and Dodie Rosekrans, the McKeons' good friends, suggested they hire Michael Taylor to finish the house. The house's ceilings, walls, and floors had to be selected, and "Taylor was so good at things like that."

ENTRANCE HALL

Marble-tiled floors in buff and antique oak paneling from an old rectory in England governed the tone for the McKeons' great hall, which was a repository for exceptional English antiques. Taylor placed an eighteenth-century console table in the style of William Kent at the fore of the interior. He mounted an elaborately carved George II gilt wood mirror above it.

Taylor's acumen and love of English antiques resulted in his locating the longest refectory table possible for the McKeons' entrance hall. He centered the imposing sixteenth-century Elizabethan oak table in the space and accessorized its top with a winsome pair of antique stone lions that he found in Cambodia. The hall's four Waterford sconces and pair of English-style brass chandeliers also echoed the vernacular of the house.

LIVING ROOM SKETCHES

Taylor called the McKeons' living room "the most comfortable room he had ever designed." But before Taylor started planning its decor, George McKeon asked him to sketch the room. Taylor acquiesced to his client's wishes, presenting him with a total of twenty color and black-and-white drawings, even though he did not like doing them. The drawings were successful. They transformed the imposing interior into a room of warmth and intimacy.

Stone urns.
Stone Table

Hooks Panel
needs Pole Table

LIVING ROOM

Taylor bathed the McKeons' living room in pale
sand-beige, creating a gentle and welcoming
backdrop for his enduring good taste. He config-
ured the room's oak-beamed ceiling, including
its hand-forged copper braces. Taylor also designed the window shutters, selecting old oak
wood for their fabrication and hand-carved
linenfold panels. He was especially grateful
that MacSweeny had procured the room's front
division of antique oak paneling from England
at the outset of the project.

The McKeons' living room reveled in a collection of notable antiques. English chairs, Chinese
tables, and Asian accessories were offset by
custom V'Soske area rugs and Taylor-designed
sofas and armchairs upholstered in Scalamandré
linen velvet. The room was also furnished with
several "California Look" pieces, such as the two-
thousand-pound stone coffee table and the pair
of rock-pile console tables that graced the
windowed seating area. Taylor was renowned for
the monumental tables which, in the McKeons'
living room, he mixed confidently with French
stone garden urns and Queen Anne mirrors from
the estate of Mona Williams von Bismarck, the
international socialite and tastemaker, and one
of Syrie Maugham's long-standing clients.

LIVING ROOM
TOWARD SCREEN

A twelve-panel coromandel screen from the estate of Norman Norell, the American fashion designer, anchored the living room's principal seating area. The vignette also included the antique Chinese coffee table and the rare George I cabriole-legged stool of walnut and parcel gilt. The sixteenth-century stool, with its upholstery of coral linen velvet, quietly introduced the decor's accent color.

DINING ROOM

Garth Benton's hand-painted Chinese wallpaper depicting a restful garden scene with flora and fauna created exoticism in the McKeons' dining room. The paper's background was cream, offset by vibrant shades of green, yellow, and peach. Benton spent several weeks at the McKeons' house completing the meticulous assignment by himself. Benton's blueprint for the wallpaper also included his signature, which he painted discreetly within the landscape's sinuous base of grass.

Taylor furnished the dining room with a custom-made dining table in subtly veined verde gris marble. The one-piece table top, which required a crew of ten to move it, was mounted to a pair of lyre-shaped stone pedestals also designed by Taylor. Although the table evoked the "California Look," it complemented the suite of baronial Queen Anne dining chairs, their fringed green velvet upholstery, and the antique Waterford crystal chandelier that Taylor purchased in Burma. The custom cream-and-green rug was by V'Soske.

DINING ROOM
TOWARD CREDENZA

The dining room's credenza and its monumental pair of carved legs were also fashioned from the same verde gris marble used for the table. The imposing sideboard, which was attached to the wall, underscored an antique Venetian wall mirror that Taylor discovered on one of his shopping expeditions. The mirror was massive and reflected the magnificence of the interior. It was also an engaging backdrop for the grouping of accessories arranged on the credenza. They included a white Chinese charger, a pair of candelabra holders with brass dolphin columns, and a collection of Famille Rose cachepots.

MR. BYRON MEYER

Byron Meyer had known Taylor for twenty years before hiring him to decorate his home. When Taylor and Mihailoff dissolved their partnership in 1954, Taylor asked Meyer, who was a successful real estate broker in San Francisco, to "find a proper retail space for him." Meyer knew that Elizabeth Arden was looking for a suitable tenant for her space at 556 Sutter Street. He called Arden at her business office in New York and brokered the deal for Taylor.

Meyer's 1930s Mediterranean-style villa on Russian Hill, which he purchased in 1974, was in dire need of a makeover. The house was decorated with "cut-pile carpet, fussy detail, and heavy velvet draperies." Meyer knew that Taylor could transform the existing interior into the appropriate backdrop for his notable and lively collection of contemporary art. Meyer wanted pared-down monochromatic interiors in the three-floor townhouse, and Taylor delivered. He specified fawn-colored walls throughout the entire house. The earth-toned paint was mixed with taping mud and applied by a trowel to the existing linen canvas walls, creating a textured finish.

LIVING ROOM

Taylor amplified the living room's monochromatic palette with varied textures and surfaces. He covered the pair of sofas and the English-style armchairs in natural-colored Indian silk, suggesting the material to Meyer because it resembled ordinary burlap. Taylor wanted "a poor look" for the interior since the economy was bad at the time. He said, "No one will ever know it's raw silk."

Meyer's living room, carpeted in sisal, was furnished with bleached Louis XV fauteuils upholstered in soft calfskin leather, occasional tables in fossil stone, and a tree-trunk table. The magnitude of the furniture, while consequential, was not typical of Taylor's usual oversized scale. He reserved that for the flourishing Ficus Benjamina trees rising from floor to ceiling and the white sandstone Régence mantel, whose depth was exaggerated "to make everything in the room bigger."

DINING ROOM

The dining room, located across the entrance hall from the living room, was furnished with Taylor's signature oak game table with cast-stone diamond-shaped pedestals modeled after the desk in his office. He paired the table with eight wicker barrel chairs cushioned in white cotton canvas. The dining room's spare backdrop, with its bleached diagonally planked oak floor, tailored moldings, and paneled window shutters, suited Meyer's art collection perfectly. It also allowed for Taylor's requisite floor-to-ceiling Ficus Benjamina trees.

MASTER BEDROOM

Meyer's bedroom, which spanned the entire width of the house, was carpeted in pale natural berber wool and furnished with a canopy bed handsomely draped and dressed in raw silk. The room was also outfitted with several distinctive pieces. They included Meyer's desk and a pair of night tables with tree-trunk bases and thick fossil stone tops. The desk was exceptional. Its legs, which were also made from thick tree trunks, supported the desk top, a gigantic eight-inch-thick slab of natural wood whose underside was hollowed out to allow seating.

PENTROOM

Taylor referred to the top floor in Meyer's house as the pentroom. The sizable lounge in the sky (Meyer's house was sited two flights above Lombard Street) proffered spectacular views of the hills of Pacific Heights and the entire Golden Gate Bridge and beyond. The grid-shuttered interior was furnished with fossil stone tables and wicker furniture cushioned in raw silk. The stone tables were extremely heavy, requiring Taylor's routine method of installation. He blocked off the intersection of Lombard Street and Larkin Street (adjacent to Meyer's house) for most of one morning while a very large heavy-duty stationary motor was positioned there. The motor, in combination with cables and a foreboding sky-hook, lifted fifteen pieces of weighty stone up the side of the house one by one. When each piece of stone reached the pentroom's west window (which had been removed), it was swung into the room through the opening and received, assembled into tables, and placed by the awaiting crew of five men, including Taylor's foreman, who directed the challenging assignment.

PRIVATE RESIDENCE

ATHERTON, CALIFORNIA, 1975

Taylor, in collaboration with Sandy Walker, attained one of his most successful collaborations with nature when they gutted and remodeled the 1950s Atherton ranch house. Key elements to the triumphant design were the expansive elevations of glass comprising the perimeter of the renovated house.

The interior decoration of the house, consisting of wicker furniture, slip-covered white cotton duck upholstery, and organic appointments, melded brilliantly with the profusion of nature pouring through the virtually invisible walls of glass. Here, Taylor did not match the decor to nature; he arranged the rooms at the core of it, creating simple and uncomplicated interiors.

LIVING ROOM

Taylor furnished the living room with wicker sofas, armchairs, and ottomans, arranging the overscaled pieces into three distinct seating areas. The two principal groupings were set against the harmonized backdrop of glass and nature, and the third one, consisting of a pair of wicker armchairs and an ottoman, bordered the fireplace. The coffee tables and the end tables, which were made from tree trunks and raw rock, furthered the living room's fervent relationship with the outdoors.

The white paper lanterns accented the living room innovatively. They were also the source of a humorous story. When Taylor presented the lanterns to his clients for their consideration, he brought three different sizes. Taylor's clients thought that the largest model of the three was too big for their living room. Taylor disagreed, telling them that the biggest one wasn't big enough. He got his clients the next largest size.

DINING ROOM

Taylor decorated the dining room simply. He
followed suit with the living room, specifying
wicker barrel dining chairs and a round pedestal
dining table that seated ten people. The table,
with its four-inch thick ash wood top, was
substantial. It was complemented by the Taylor-
designed travertine sideboard also serving the
room. The two contiguous walls of glass
afforded a generous view of the surrounding
property.

MR. GIL GARFIELD

Gil Garfield, the prominent songwriter and businessman, admired Taylor's work long before he hired Taylor to decorate his house. Garfield was gripped by a photograph of Taylor's work he saw in a magazine in 1970 and wrote to him, uncharacteristically, to say how much he admired his talent, and if he ever had something to decorate, he would hire him. He also mentioned in the letter he wanted to meet Taylor. Taylor personally telephoned Garfield shortly after receiving the flattering note and thanked him for writing it. He introduced himself to Garfield over the phone as "Michael," but Garfield didn't recognize his voice and responded, "I know a lot of Michaels, Michael who?" Taylor identified himself again to Garfield, saying, "This is Michael Taylor."

Garfield and Taylor hit it off instantly, and they finally met when Taylor, who visited Los Angeles often, went to Garfield's house for a drink and to see how he lived. The two men recognized and appreciated each other's creativity and realized they would work together on a project one day. That day came in 1976, when Garfield purchased a forward-looking house designed in 1950 by Harwell Hamilton Harris (1903–1990), the influential Modernist architect.

Taylor approached the Garfield project in his usual way. First, he "lived the rooms" of the house, spending quality time in them at various intervals over a two-day period. Taylor closely monitored the sources of natural light, which always governed his methodology for each individual project. He "knew what the key elements had to be by being in the space."

Garfield recalls Taylor and Bob Burdine visiting the house at the outset of the project. Taylor was there to contemplate the interiors and rhapsodically conduct Burdine through each room while Burdine sketched Taylor's ideas on drafting paper as they percolated and evolved in Taylor's mind. Burdine sketched away, but it was Taylor's creative genius controlling his pace, his arm, and his hand.

Garfield's assignment coincided with Taylor's initiation of the "Jennifer" line of furniture and his customary use of concrete and river rocks in his interiors. Harris had designed the house in accordance with its resplendent surroundings. His sculptural architecture and the colorless rooms Taylor created for the house would be harmonious.

LIVING ROOM

Taylor furnished Garfield's expansive living room with "Jennifer" wicker chairs and ottomans cushioned in white cotton twill. He grouped the over-scaled pieces with river rock tables and exceptionally tall trees towering toward the room's twenty-eight-foot ceiling and its shoji-like skylight. Taylor also completely mirrored one of the principal walls in the living room, enabling significant interaction between the organic interior and its reflections of nature with its evolving breadth of colors through the wall of windows overlooking the terrace. The center panel of glass, which retracted electronically into the wall, also advanced the relationship between the indoors and the outdoors.

DINING ROOM

A solid concrete dining table that Taylor designed anchored the dining room. The table seated fourteen people, weighed three thousand pounds, and required structural reinforcement with large beams in the house's wine cellar below. The accompanying director's chairs, upholstered in ordinary white cotton duck, perpetuated the informality of Taylor's decor. They also symbolized his versatility. Taylor purchased the chairs for twenty-seven dollars apiece at Pier One Imports.

MR. ALFRED WILSEY
MS. PAT MONTANDON

When Alfred Wilsey and Pat Montandon commissioned Porter and Steinwedell to design the house for River Meadow Farm in the Napa Valley, they asked for a design that was "something purely American." The end result was a house of clapboard and stone with a gabled wood-shake roof. *House & Garden*, which featured the Rutherford commission on two consecutive covers of the magazine, branded the interiors "Country Modern."

LIVING ROOM

Vibrant colors and glossy lacquered surfaces created a cheerful living room for Wilsey and Montandon. Especially uplifting to the decor was the French lemon chintz upholstery patterned predominantly in pink and rose tulips. Taylor also made the room's swagged curtains from the chintz, including the pair framing the book-lined alcove and its window seat.

The scarlet lacquered tables also enlivened the living room. Their polished luster was potent, and it only intensified the vitality of the lemon-yellow color scheme. The towering pair of fishtail palms, the Giacometti-style plaster lamps, and the Cost Plus wicker pieces outfitting the room symbolized several of Taylor's favorite appurtenances.

MASTER BEDROOM

Taylor infused vivid color into the master bedroom. He draped the canopy bed and upholstered most of the furniture in hot-peony-pink
and blush-white checked linen. Taylor also designed the room's needlepoint rug, basing its
bold and generous pattern of flowers and shells
on the original diminutive model. The Frances
Elkins bedside loop chair and the Giacometti-
style night-table lamps reiterated Taylor's
adoration of the two influential designers.

MASTER BEDROOM FIREPLACE

The roll-arm sofa fronting the canopied bed, the
pair of Syrie Maugham armchairs, and the fireside ottoman composed a cozy and comfortable
sitting area in the master bedroom. Taylor
considered the bedroom perfect. Given the
opportunity, he would have not changed anything in the room. *House & Garden* shared his
sentiment; the magazine featured this photo
on the cover of their January 1978 issue.

MR. AND MRS. GARY FAMILIAN

BRENTWOOD, CALIFORNIA, 1978

Gary and Liz Familian were long-standing clients of Taylor's. He decorated five houses for them, including the first house he collaborated on with John Lautner. Gil Garfield brought Taylor to the attention of the Familians, as well as several other of his friends who also hired Taylor to decorate their houses.

The Familian's Brentwood house, thirty years old and traditional, was Taylor's third commission for them. They asked him, along with Jerrold Lomax, the prominent West Coast architect, to pare down the interior, transforming it into a clean-lined contemporary space.

Liz Familian, like Garfield, marveled at Taylor in action. He mapped furniture plans right in the rooms he was decorating for her and her family, directing his assistants—usually Bob Burdine and Chuck Husted—to cut out trial facsimiles of the furniture from a large roll of construction paper they brought to the site and rolled out on the floor of each room. Taylor and his staff then arranged the facsimiles on the floor where they moved, adjusted, or recut them according to Taylor's instinctive sense of what was right for the particular space.

Taylor also initiated Gary and Liz Familians' collection of contemporary art, advising them as new clients to purchase paintings instead of consenting to the ridiculously high bid to wallpaper their house. He told the Familians, "We'll paint the walls white and visit my friend Nick Wilder." Gary and Liz Familian purchased several paintings from Wilder, always appreciating the prescient guidance they received from Taylor

LIVING ROOM BY FIREPLACE

"Jennifer" furniture in faux stone comprised the seating area by the living room fireplace. The pair of chairs and the ottoman, which were extremely comfortable and roomy, perpetuated the organic sensibility of Taylor's design. The tall flax plants flanking the fireplace and the blooming pink hydrangea accenting the coffee table made the monochromatic interior come alive according to Taylor's premeditated plan.

LIVING ROOM

Taylor created a living room for the Familians that was crisp and clean. He painted most of the room white and mirrored its principal wall to reflect the house's newly designed gardens, making them key to his minimalist design scheme. Unadorned doors and windows enabled the natural colors from the outdoors to infiltrate the living room without interruption.

The living room's organic surfaces, natural finishes, and white cotton duck upholstery also attracted the exterior color palette. Although the room's banquette was capacious, its light fabric and recessed base gave its presence a weightless quality. The angular travertine coffee table and balancing pair of wicker ottomans also floated within the space.

MR. AND MRS. MARC NATHANSON

BEVERLY HILLS, CALIFORNIA, 1978

Marc and Jane Nathanson asked Taylor to create a subtly elegant and indestructible environment for their Spanish hacienda-style house, where they were raising three children. Taylor responded diligently to their request, incorporating concrete, wood, and rock into the 1920s house and its newly built family room designed by Peter Choate.

LIVING ROOM

The redecoration of the Nathansons' living room included a pair of Taylor's sleek cement-based banquettes cushioned in one of his favorite fabrics: Kravet ribbed cotton. He upholstered all the seating in the spacious room in the white textured fabric, including the balanced pair of banquettes innovatively built into the fireplace's newly conceived cement hearth.

Organic elements—a tree-trunk table, a wicker planter and armchair, and an eighteenth-century Mexican coffee table on the stepped cement platform—also added character to the living room. The sophisticated rusticity of the decor complemented the Nathansons' notable collection of contemporary art.

FAMILY ROOM

Taylor expanded upon his clients' requisites
when he decorated the family room. He paved
the entire addition in Yosemite slate and
arranged it with overscaled furniture that was
completely indestructible.

The principal seating area in the family room
consisted of a long built-in banquette running
along the wall the entire length of the room.
The banquette, which formed an L on both of
its ends, was based in cement and cushioned in
Kravet ribbed cotton. Taylor purposely aligned
one L with the fireplace hearth, incorporating
the raw rock component as one of the
banquette's end tables.

The family room was also furnished with
"Jennifer" furniture in white faux stone,
including a pair of the overscaled chairs. They,
too, were slipcovered in white ribbed cotton and
grouped similarly with raw rock tables. Taylor
was partial to the distinctive organic formations.
He recessed two of them partway into the fireplace's plastered wall, creating a mantelpiece
that was innovative and coherent with the
room's design scheme.

FAMILY ROOM TOWARD
THE SWIMMING POOL

The family room was planned in sync with the
outdoors. Its engaging view of the pool area was
framed by a "Jennifer" chair and an ash pedestal
games table with Philippine rattan chairs
designed by Taylor. The pair of eleven-foot-tall
glass pocket doors created nominal separation
between the family room's interior and the
exterior surroundings, where contemporary
sculpture from the Nathansons' art collection
was displayed.

MR. AND MRS. ROBERT PHILLIPS

YOUNTVILLE, CALIFORNIA, 1978

Gardner Dailey (1895–1967), the prominent San Francisco architect, designed Bob and Alex Phillips's Napa Valley house in 1959 for Bruce and Grace Kelham—Alex's parents. When the Phillipses moved into the contemporary house on a full-time basis in 1978 (they had purchased the house from Alex's family), they hired Taylor to redecorate its summer room. The great room was used only during the months of May through October. Vale Kasper decorated the house for the Kelhams, who spent weekends and summers there.

SUMMER ROOM

The summer room was designed as an indoor-outdoor room. It opened on to the swimming pool and the garden designed by Thomas Church (1902–1978), the renowned San Francisco landscape architect.

Taylor specified a white interior for the Phillipses, furnishing it with overscaled furniture, stone tables, and wicker chairs and ottomans from Cost Plus. He also filled the room with giant fiddle-leaf fig trees and installed Charles Arnoldi's Grasshopper tree-branch wall sculpture above the seating area's sofa.

The sofa, which was upholstered in white cotton duck, was enormous. But before Taylor designed the piece of furniture and had it made, he delivered to the Phillipses a model one-half the size of its ultimate thirteen-foot length. He wanted Bob and Alex to see what felt good to them.

SUMMER ROOM TOWARD
THE SWIMMING POOL

Dailey created comfortable access between the
summer room and the terrace surrounding the
swimming pool. He designed three sets of French
pocket doors that united the two environments
easily and framed a view of the mountains. Taylor
liked the balanced arrangement of the doors.
It influenced his symmetrical blueprint for
the room.

Taylor was particularly enthusiastic about the
summer room's existing mirrors and pair of
marble-topped console tables that came from
Grace Kelham's house in Woodside. He told Alex
that she had to "bring them up here because they
handled the mirrors well." The regal tables, which
were purchased by Alex's grandmother at Jansen
of Paris, also "handled" the wicker ottomans and
the soy tubs that Taylor bought at Cost Plus (soy
tubs were dark brown, glazed, onion-shaped pots
that originally contained soy sauce).

SUMMER ROOM TOWARD
THE ARBOR

Taylor fabricated the summer room's principal
tables from stone, including the balanced pair of
octagonal pedestal games tables and the ten-foot-
long cocktail table with its Greek capital legs. The
wicker armchairs and the bamboo cigarette tables
came from Cost Plus. Taylor liked the emporium
pieces. He felt that their simplicity and natural
patina intimated that Alex had found them in
her grandmother's attic.

MR. AND MRS. TOBY SCHREIBER

WOODSIDE, CALIFORNIA, 1978

The Woodside commission was another successful collaboration between Michael Taylor and Sandy Walker. Walker designed the modern one-level house for Toby and Rita Schreiber. The sprawling masterpiece, with its massive windows, tall ceilings, and ample wall space, showcased the Schreibers' important collection of contemporary art.

LIVING ROOM

Taylor created a background of soft white in the Schreibers' living room, allowing the art to be the focal point and the primary source of color. He arranged the room with a suite of substantial wicker furniture that was custom-designed and cushioned in white cotton duck. The two large sofas were modeled after the "Jennifer" prototype.

Fossilized stone, smooth leather, and glazed ceramic tile were also indicative of Taylor's design philosophy. All three elements contributed textured patina to the room without imposing on the museum-quality art lit by special lighting designed by Taylor and MacMasters.

MS. PAT MONTANDON

SAN FRANCISCO, CALIFORNIA, 1979

Taylor applied his architectural skill to Pat Montandon's penthouse duplex on Russian Hill. Initially, he removed every interior wall on the first floor of the spacious aerie. Taylor also eliminated the atrium, expanding the footprint of the apartment's main floor, which he paved entirely in pinkish-beige travertine. His specification of soft beige walls with strategically placed divisions of mirror also amplified the space and integrated it with the pulsating views seen from the bay-side floor-to-ceiling wall of glass.

LIVING ROOM BY TAPESTRY

The living room's principal seating area, which faced the fireplace, was juxtaposed against a backdrop of mirrored walls and an expansive Belgian tapestry. Softly textured fabrics in gradations of pale beige covered the sofa and the suite of Taylor-designed bleached Régence chairs, perpetuating clarity in the plant-laden interior. Taylor's signature look was also symbolized by the large travertine coffee table fronting the sofa. According to Coby Everdell, installing the travertine table in the apartment was a feat unto itself. Taylor had purposely invited Everdell to the site on the day of the install. He wanted Everdell to see examples of his furniture in anticipation of his decorating the villa in Saudi Arabia.

Everdell arrived at Montandon's building to witness the coffee table dangling like a kite over Russian Hill, a spectacle that was visible to Everdell several blocks away from the site. The table had been rigged at ground level to a cable running up the side of the building before terminating in Montandon's living room, where it was bolted to the ceiling. When the table reached the thirty-second floor of the building, it was maneuvered into the apartment through a large opening in the glass wall where two windows had been removed expressly for the installation. Once the table was safely inside the apartment, Taylor's awaiting foreman and crew of twelve men carried it to its precise location.

LIVING ROOM FIREPLACE

Taylor outfitted the living room's fireplace with a
French sandstone mantel. He also mirrored the
chimneybreast, diffusing reflections exponentially throughout the glamorous interior. Inspiring visions of the towering Ficus Benjamina
trees, the Roman and pre-Columbian artifacts,
and everything else created by Taylor's ingenuity
abounded wherever the eye traveled.

LIVING ROOM BY STAIRCASE

Taylor floated various seating areas throughout
the first floor of Montandon's apartment. He
placed a Louis XVI chinoiserie tray table and a
flanking pair of his custom Régence chairs alongside the duplex's freestanding circular staircase.
The bleached-oak staircase, with its open treads
and railings, swept gracefully to the apartment's
second floor, blending inconspicuously with the
copious arrangements of twenty-five-foot-tall
Ficus Benjamina trees.

SITTING AREA BY THE BAY

A mixture of faux-stone "Jennifer" furniture
and a pair of rattan chairs and bamboo cigarette
tables from Cost Plus outfitted the bayside
division of the apartment, where the atrium
once stood. Hand-cut basket-weave chenille
iin pale beige (the same fabric used on the living
room sofa) covered all the upholstered pieces.
The overhanging Ficus Benjamina tree and the
commanding views seen through the floor-to-
ceiling wall of glass diminished the distinction
between the indoors and the outdoors—
even on the thirty-second floor.

GAMES TABLE BY THE BAY

Taylor anchored the living room's northeast corner with a travertine pedestal games table. Four
bleached Régence chairs served the octagonal
table, providing additional seating for Montandon's luncheon and dinner guests. The apartment's dining table, which sat in balance to the
games table on the opposite side of the sitting
area, also overlooked San Francisco Bay.

DINING AREA

The profusion of flourishing plants and flowers, including the Ficus Benjamina, the raspberry-colored sedum, and the sprays of red kangaroo paws, composed a lush backdrop in Montandon's dining area. The travertine pedestal dining table and console, although they were extremely heavy, appeared visually weightless in the airy, light-filled setting.

MR. AND MRS. JOHN N. ROSEKRANS JR.

SAN FRANCISCO, CALIFORNIA, 1980

ATRIUM

Taylor was enthused with the Rosekranses'
atrium. The monumental space appealed to his
mutual appreciation of sizable scale and the outdoors. Lentelli's ornate carvings—in concert with
the villa's seasoned architecture—were an ideal
backdrop for Taylor's copious arrangement of
gigantic palm trees.

SMOKING ROOM

Taylor's triumph with the Rosekrans commission was especially prominent in the smoking room. Here, monochromatic color, gutsy textures, and unique objects created a primitive but highly sophisticated interior. Grass cloth in a pale golden hue covered the walls; the sofa and a pair of lounge chairs were upholstered in custom-woven tobacco linen. A stone capital end table, an arrangement of immense Brazilian quartz crystals, and a travertine-topped coffee table broadcast the Taylor look. African art and organic sculpture added dimension to the room. Taylor installed one of a pair of majestic carved wooden Senufo birds on each side of the sofa and mounted a Charles Arnoldi tree-branch sculpture on the wall behind it. Taylor favored Arnoldi's work because it was natural. He enthusiastically promoted Arnoldi's work to his clients and placed it in many of their homes. The Rosekranses' smoking room was one of Taylor's favorite interiors.

DINING ROOM

Lentelli's classical detailing in the dining room
and the living room formed an effective backdrop for Taylor's interior decoration of the two
state rooms. In the dining room, a monumental
pair of fluted pilasters with tailored bases and
ornate capitals framed the fireplace mantel.
The mantel, fabricated in white marble, complemented Taylor's custom-designed dining table.
The table, with its three-inch-thick, ninety-inch-
round white travertine top, accommodated a
suite of eight straight-back English hall chairs.
Rosekrans purchased six of the chairs at the
Clark auction, and when she moved to the new
house Taylor had the additional pair made. The
dining room was enhanced by its commanding
view of San Francisco Bay. By day, northern light
filtered through the room's windowed wall and
glistened in the rock-crystal drops of the
eighteenth-century French chandelier that
dangled over the dining table like a crown jewel.
The chandelier had originally hung in the
Paris apartment of Maria Callas.

LIVING ROOM

The living room, which was connected to the dining room, was the third and largest room within the sequence of the main rooms. It also overlooked the Bay through a pair of arched French doors. The doors opened onto an expansive balustraded terrace that spanned the entire back of the house. An eclectic collection of outstanding furniture and accessories defined the living room. The mixture of pieces included a muted eighteenth-century Samarkand carpet, which defined the principal seating area. Here, Taylor arranged a large-scale sofa against the backdrop of a late seventeenth-century twelve-panel coromandel screen. The sofa, with its plump pillows and bouillon cord fringe skirting, was upholstered in custom-woven Belgian linen in golden straw. Yellow was the living room's primary accent color. The soft golden color also suited the gaufrage Mozart velvet in chartreuse covering the quartet of gilded scroll-armed chairs. Only one of the eighteenth-century William Kent chairs was original. Taylor purchased it from Rose Cumming. He made the additional chairs for the Rosekranses.

LIVING ROOM TOWARD FIREPLACE

Taylor also created a pair of balanced seating areas at the fireplace wall, directly opposite the screened wall. On each side of the fireplace he placed a sofa and an eighteenth-century black-lacquered mother-of-pearl and eggshell Chinese coffee table. The sofas, upholstered in golden straw woven linen and decoratively finished in nail-head trim, were modeled after one that belonged to Elsa Schiaparelli, the Parisian fashion designer. A set of six lavishly gilded Russian armchairs contributed opulence. The chairs, with gracefully concave solid wood backs, elaborately carved and detailed elbow rests, cabriole legs, and carved lion-paw feet, were regal. They took a position of prominence in this room of beautiful objects.

MASTER BEDROOM

The Rosekranses' master bedroom was dramatic.
The room was first set up in Taylor's Sutter Street
shop in 1960. The vignette was also featured in
Vogue's September 1960 "Fashions in Living"
article, "The Colour Directions." The focal point
of the bedroom was the carved eighteenth-century Portuguese canopy bed with its jet-black
corkscrew posts. It was curtained in heavy
oyster-white homespun nylon. The original
pale-white bedding was changed to black
satin when the bedroom was installed in the
Rosekranses' first home.

MASTER BEDROOM TOWARD FIREPLACE

Taylor created a balanced tableau along the
intricately detailed fireplace wall. He offset
the marble mantel with a pair of tufted wide
armchairs, which also came from the
Rosekranses' original bedroom. The armchairs and the accompanying ottoman were
upholstered in oyster-white nylon.

MR. DOUGLAS S. CRAMER

SANTA YNEZ, CALIFORNIA, 1980

LIVING ROOM

Taylor convinced Cramer to decorate La Quinta with a preference for American Southwest and Mediterranean sensibilities—styles that were new to Cramer. He gave the interiors a neutral backdrop of sophisticated rusticity. The floors throughout the house were paved in Yosemite slate, and the majority of the furniture was built into each room. In the living room, the over-scaled sofa and chairs were made of plaster and outfitted with cushions in natural Haitian cotton, one of the two hundred fabric samples considered by Taylor and Cramer for the living room and library. Black granite–topped tables and stone capital tables completed the seating arrangements.

Although Cramer's living room was composed primarily of "California Look" furniture designed by Taylor specifically for the commission, it was also embellished with an extremely rare Irish refectory table the two men spotted in a London antiques shop during one of their joint trips to Europe. Taylor and Cramer shopped for choice antiques throughout London, Paris, Rome, and Madrid over a period of many months. Taylor's careful placement of the pieces they selected in Cramer's house "created timelessness" in the interiors.

DINING ROOM

Taylor designed the ranch's dining room following the Southwestern vernacular. He nestled an adobe-style fireplace into one of the room's corners and beamed its whitewashed planked ceiling. The ash wood-topped dining table and its caned tree-branch armchairs accommodated twelve guests.

MASTER BEDROOM

Cramer's master bedroom was a retreat unto itself. The large suite was on two levels. It contained a book-lined loft that opened onto an outdoor terrace and also overlooked the bedroom's sitting area. Natural fabrics in a pale-beige weave covered all the room's upholstered pieces, including the three ash-framed log-and-rush armchairs that Taylor aptly named the Douglas chair—after Cramer.

TERRACE

Life at La Quinta Norte was also about the outdoors. A large terrace extended the length of the
house. Taylor outfitted the outdoor seating area
with his custom-designed teak furniture. Cramer
and his guests relaxed here, overlooking his
ranch, his Douglas Vineyards, and the complex
man-made waterfalls that ran through the house
before cascading down the terraced hillside into
two pools twenty feet apart—also suggested
by Taylor.

MR. CHARLES EVANS

NEW YORK, NEW YORK, 1980

When Taylor decorated Charles Evans's Park Avenue apartment, he did the living room—twice. On the first occasion, Taylor was auditioning for his prospective client, thanks to Nan Kempner, who lived in the building where Evans, the executive producer of the film *Tootsie*, had just purchased the penthouse triplex. She told her soon-to-be neighbor, "When you get to furnishing your apartment, you must have Michael Taylor take a look at it." Evans "didn't know who he was."

Taylor was in New York three to four times a month. During one of these visits, he called on Evans at his current apartment. Coincidentally, Evans lived across the street from the Regency Hotel—where Taylor always stayed when he was in the city. The two men chatted, and Taylor got a feel for how Evans lived. One hour later, they were at the triplex—only a five-minute taxi-cab ride from Evans's home.

Evans walked Taylor around the bare apartment, sharing some of his opinions about the place with him before leaving for a one o'-clock meeting. Taylor, whose ideas were already percolating as he measured the scale of each room by "putting his thumb up in the air," asked Evans if he could stay. Evans said yes, and Taylor got to work. Six hours later, he called Evans at his office. Taylor "had a few ideas," and asked Evans "if he could come up now."

When Evans walked into the apartment he "couldn't believe it." Taylor "had furnished the living room." Taylor, along with a friend he summoned to the apartment, mocked up the complete furniture plan with cheese boxes and cardboard models they had made. Taylor also simulated a grand piano with an open top. He propped up one large cardboard box on top of another, using a tall stick to hold them apart.

Taylor appointed the living room beautifully. He accessorized the cheese-box tables with lit candles and plants and flowers from the corner florist. He even feigned a sculpture at one of the windows, crushing a section of the *New York Times* to create the mass. Evans, who was duly impressed with the resourceful and extraordinary presentation, shook hands with Taylor and told him, "You've got a job." Taylor's timing was ideal. Evans had planned to "give it to another decorator that very day."

LIVING ROOM

Taylor arranged and appointed Evans's living room "just as he had done the mock-up," creating a monochromatic backdrop for the spare and sophisticated interior. He washed the well-proportioned room in greige, the distinctive gray-beige palette "that all the Parisian fashion salons were done in."

The living room's decor was planned in harmony with the natural light and the generous city views seen through its multiple banks of windows, purposely left without shades or curtains. The bleached oak floors were also bare, and the fabric-covered walls were completely unadorned. Neutral tones pervaded the living room furniture as well. The modern rounded sofas were upholstered in oatmeal wool flannel, and similarly hued raw silk covered the suite of four bleached Régence fauteuils. Taylor accented Evans's living room with the "California Look." He paved the fireplace wall in beige travertine and fabricated the low coffee tables from the identical stone. The adroit use of the travertine, combined with the room's strategic arrangements of flowering plants and towering potted trees, demonstrated that the West Coast aesthetic was bicoastal.

MR. AND MRS. GORHAM B. KNOWLES

SAN FRANCISCO, CALIFORNIA, 1981

ENTRANCE GALLERY

Taylor anchored the fore of the Knowles's entrance gallery with an eighteenth-century-style gilt gesso pier table, an antique gilt tole wall mirror, and a pair of carved and painted Louis XV consoles, foreshadowing the pedigreed collection of antiques furnishing the sixteen-room house.

The middle division of the beamed gallery was distinguished by an outstanding K'ang Shi twelve-fold coromandel screen. It was fronted by a white painted and gilded banquette stool upholstered in tomato-colored velvet. The monumental stone staircase at the far end of the gallery, balanced by an ancient Romanesque granite baptistery, ascended the natural light-flooded stairwell, equally reminiscent of an outdoor garden venue. The indoor-outdoor effect that appeared frequently throughout the house was prioritized by Taylor and Porter and Steinwedell in their remodeling plans for the Knowleses.

SITTING AREA

The sitting area materialized when Porter and Steinwedell suggested incorporating a library into the gallery's expansive footprint. Taylor objected vehemently to the idea, insisting on having an "impressive" gallery. Although he told the architects to "put the library upstairs," Diana Knowles convinced all three of them to "have a sitting area" in the first-floor space.

Knowles's suggestion resulted in an open and airy venue accommodating many guests during the sizable cocktail parties hosted by her and her husband. The sitting area, separated from the gallery solely by a seventeenth-century Chinese black-lacquer and gold altar table, was also furnished with several pieces from the Jackson Street house, including the settee, the French Empire ormolu bouillotte tables, and the pair of eighteenth-century Italian marble-topped tables flanking the antique French stone fireplace mantel. The sitting area, which was the third living room on the house's first floor, opened fittingly into the dining room.

DINING ROOM

Taylor furnished the Knowleses' dining room against the elegant backdrop of hand-painted Chinese wallpaper and antique parquet-de-Versailles he purchased long distance, by telephone, when it was auctioned in France. The French parquet, which came from a palace and was originally installed on sand, was leveled and coated with cork and bitual before it was placed in the Knowleses' dining room.

The wallpaper, with its bird and floral motif, was exquisite. It was composed of fourteen original eighteenth-century panels "repaired, restored, and extended" by Art Fine—the talented Los Angeles artist.

Gorham and Diana Knowles enjoyed their new dining room, which effortlessly accommodated many guests. Although the English mahogany oval dining table, the Louis XVI cane-backed dining chairs, and the French crystal chandelier all came from the Jackson Street house, Taylor acquired the early eighteenth-century French provincial walnut enfilade expressly for the new dining room. The thirteen-foot-long six-door buffet, with its galbe and parquet top, originally outfitted the Chateaux Les Roches in France. The large eighteenth-century sandstone garden urns anchoring each of the dining room's corners displayed prized orchids from Diana Knowles's off-premises greenhouse.

GARDEN ROOM

The idea for the Knowleses' garden room was initiated when their soon-to-be Presidio Heights neighbors were "incensed" at the architects' plan to "enclose the front garden behind a twenty-foot wall." Diana Knowles, never to be dissuaded by resistance, "had another brilliant idea." She suggested having a garden room instead of a garden extending from the house's entrance gallery. The newly built room would also connect with the living room, creating ideal circulation on the first floor of the house.

Taylor and Porter and Steinwedell agreed with Knowles. Together they envisioned a corbel-walled garden room of exemplary proportions, flooded generously with natural light through skylit panels of mullioned glass recessed into its beamed ceiling.

The Knowleses' garden room was one of Taylor's most triumphant indoor-outdoor executions. He furnished the interior in casual opulence, anchoring each of its skylit corners with a nine-foot-tall French stone caryatid, which together depicted the four continents of America, Asia, Africa, and Europe. The eighteenth-century garden statuary was imposing. It stood as a sentry to Taylor's adept and aptly scaled arrangement of furniture, starting with the garden room's seating area.

Taylor furnished the seating area commodiously. He outfitted its skylit corbelled alcove with an overscaled thirteen-and-one-half-foot banquette upholstered in Brunschwig & Fils Serin (gold) Mozart velvet. The accompanying inlaid marble coffee table, the flanking Louis XV-style pale-green painted bergères, and the stone capital side tables imbued eclecticism into the gardenlike setting.

The garden room was also conceived for intimate dining and bridge games because, when Knowles "saw her guests playing bridge in the hall" of the Jackson Street house, she couldn't bear seeing "everyone milling around" like it was a railway station. The garden room, with its nineteenth-century lacquered games table and round travertine table for four, completely mollified Knowles's discontent.

LIVING ROOM

The extensive compilation of antiques for the Knowleses' new house reached its pinnacle in the living room, where museum-quality French, English, and Chinese pieces mingled harmoniously with the balanced pair of Schiaparelli-style sofas custom-made by Taylor and also upholstered luxuriously in Brunschwig & Fils Serin Mozart velvet.

On the living room's principal wall, the seventeenth-century French stone fireplace with trumeau was balanced by a pair of George II painted side tables from Wardour Castle near Tisbury, in the English county of Wiltshire, and an accompanying pair of eighteenth-century Venetian pier mirrors. Taylor purchased the eighteenth-century tables for the Knowleses long distance, by telephone, when Christies auctioned them at the spectacular Luttrellstown Castle sale in Ireland. He also purchased at auction from Sotheby Parke Bernet numerous pieces from the Palm Beach, Florida, residence of Jayne Wrightsman (Mrs. Charles), including the pair of eighteenth-century Régence gilt wood chaises à la reine offset by the fireplace.

Taylor and Knowles were reciprocally partial
to French chairs, and Chinese and chinoiserie
furniture for the living room. Fortunately,
together they located and acquired a suite of six
mid-eighteenth-century Louis XV bergères, each
upholstered in its original petit-point floral
tapestry. Taylor and Knowles also found several
black lacquered pieces, purchasing many of them
at auction. They included the black-and-gold
japanned sofa table and the eighteenth-century
Italian chinoiserie-decorated chest of drawers,
surmounted by an eighteenth-century Queen
Anne wall mirror.

Diana Knowles has loved everything she
acquired with Taylor. In fact, she recalled in 2006
that "everything I have here is Michael Taylor.
It looks just as good today as the day I bought it."

GUEST SUITES

The Knowleses' third-floor guest suites were enchanting. The pink bedroom, with its spectacular view of San Francisco Bay seen through the new oval dormer window, was decorated in a Manuel Canovas cotton print. The pair of country French chairs, the ottoman, and Taylor's twist-and-column floor lamp comprised a cozy sitting area alongside the bedroom's Louis XV stone fireplace.

The overall application of toile de Jouy wall-covering amplified the blue-and-white bedroom and accentuated its unusual configuration. Taylor outfitted the bedroom with a sleigh bed, dressing it as well in the quilted toile. The eighteenth-century painted French walnut daybed and the Louis XV caned and painted fauteuil de cabinet, also purchased at the Wrightsman auction, furthered the bedroom's charm.

MR. AND MRS. WARREN SPIEKER JR.

SAN FRANCISCO, CALIFORNIA, 1981

ENTRANCE HALL

Taylor created the illusion of limitless space by
mirroring the Spiekers' white travertine entrance
hall. The designer also dramatized the hallway
by using a focal intricately carved pine console
table and overscaled Michael Taylor Designs
stone urn. The Lucite bench, with its seat in
beige herringbone chenille, was practically
transparent.

LIVING ROOM

The apartment's living room was cool white, accented with shades of apple green. Taylor favored green because it represented nature. He diffused the color effectively throughout the interior with several Brunschwig & Fils silk fabrics. They included vibrant striped taffeta-covered pillows lining the room's overscaled U-shaped sofa and balancing pair of banquettes, mutually upholstered in Kravet white ribbed cotton.

LIVING ROOM AT DESK

Taylor furnished the living room with several pieces of travertine furniture he designed; the Jean-Michel Frank–style parsons desk anchoring a corner of the room, and the pair of coffee tables serving the sofa and the banquettes. Taylor's design for the coffee tables was especially innovative. He set their thick cove-edged stone tops on mirrored cube bases, making them visually weightless. Taylor applied the same design strategy to the living room's pair of Lucite-based stools, which also floated on the white V'-Soske wool rug.

DINING ROOM

The apartment's dining room was spare and eclectic. The view-side room, with its bare travertine floor, was furnished with a large round pedestal dining table, also in travertine, and a suite of six Regency-style armchairs, cushioned in apple-green woven silk. The color green, which complemented the dining room, was emphasized by the potted Sparmania Africana plants flourishing throughout the interior. Taylor spotted the exotic tropical-like evergreens while driving through Golden Gate Park, telling his full-time gardener that "we have to get those trees for Spieker's apartment; their leaves match the acid green of the taffeta stripe pillows."

MR. AND MRS. ALFRED S. WILSEY

SAN FRANCISCO, CALIFORNIA, 1982

LIVING ROOM

The Wilsey's formal living room was set up with a large eighteenth-century Aubusson carpet that Dede purchased in Peru. The carpet, with its restful shades of pink, ecru, and touches of green, governed the tone for the pale-pink room. Elegantly appointed with Impressionist art and fine antiques, the room contained fourteen yards of billowing Scalamandré green, yellow, pink, and ecru striped silk-taffeta curtains.

LIVING ROOM

Taylor followed one of his "old secrets for furniture arranging" in the living room. He created three zones of seating. He placed a roll-arm sofa of his own design on the principal wall. The sofa, which was sumptuously upholstered in hand-cut embossed emerald-green silk velvet, offset a gilded eighteenth-century Venetian table and a screen with hand-painted Chinese panels set into custom-carved gilded frames. A lustrous pair of square chinoiserie coffee tables, an over-sized wing chair, and a Taylor-designed Louis XVI–style armchair completed the vignette. Both chairs were upholstered in subtly textured fabrics in soft yellow.

LIVING ROOM AT FIREPLACE

A Schiaparelli sofa covered in peridot velvet anchored each of the seating areas framing the fireplace. The balanced seating areas were intimate. They were both augmented by a Taylor-designed Louis XVI-style armchair and a stone elephant table. The tables, which tempered the formality of the room, reflected Taylor's design aesthetic. Although he intimated to Wilsey that her tables had come from India, they were undoubtedly purchased at Cost Plus. Taylor, who always gave his clients "a great spiel" on a piece of furniture, was protective of his sources.

DINING ROOM

The Wilseys' dining room glowed with yellow lacquered walls, mirrored panels, and a mirrored screen that reflected the choice selection of antiques. The mahogany dining table was English. The eighteenth-century Waterford crystal chandelier came from a palace in India. A suite of twelve hand-painted Italian chairs upholstered in lime-green cotton ottoman fabric was arranged around the table and interspersed along the perimeter of the room. Although Taylor dressed each of the four windows with thinly striped yellow silk-taffeta curtains, he incorporated Lucite curtain rods and his signature matchstick shades along with the luxuriant window treatment.

GARDEN ROOM

Taylor aligned the garden room's spacious seating area with the connecting living room. He arranged it around a substantial coffee table whose seventeenth-century Italian marble inlaid top was originally a console table. Taylor readapted the tall stone legs for the travertine console table also installed in the garden room. The inlaid marble coffee table complemented the balanced suite of overstuffed upholstered pieces: a large sofa and four comfortable armchairs upholstered in white Crowder basket-weave chenille. The pieces were skirted generously in white bouillon cord fringe. The ormolu gueridon next to the sofa was topped in malachite.

GARDEN ROOM DINING AREA

Taylor accented the garden room with Wilsey's favorite color. He upholstered the seat cushions of the six black-lacquered Directoire chairs in pink silk. The chairs, with their subtly gilt-decorated frames, were classic. They coexisted flawlessly with Taylor's round travertine-topped dining table. The table sat near the wall of glass that overlooked the balustraded balcony and San Francisco Bay.

MS. EILEEN McKEON

SAN FRANCISCO, CALIFORNIA,
1982

Eileen McKeon, George and Elaine McKeon's daughter, hired Taylor, in collaboration with Sandy Walker, to remodel the Victorian house she purchased on Russian Hill. The two-bedroom house typified the late nineteenth century, with its dark interiors and warren of small rooms. Fortunately, Victorian houses had tall ceilings.

The first enhancement Taylor and Walker made to the house was removing its rear wall and replacing it with French doors. This allowed natural light to pour into the interiors, which Taylor lightened further when he painted them creamy white. McKeon's house contained some of the smallest rooms ever decorated by Taylor. He made them feel large, regardless of the limitation, with overscaled furniture.

LIVING ROOM

Taylor decorated the living room monochromatically, anchoring it with an earth-toned cotton dhurrie rug and covering all the upholstered pieces, which he designed, in natural-colored linen velvet.

The living room's principal seating, a melon-shaped ottoman and four encircling English-style club chairs, was oriented toward the fireplace and its enhancing mirrored wall. Reflected colors from the room's display of contemporary art complemented Taylor's restful design scheme.

MASTER BEDROOM
AND SITTING ROOM

Taylor told McKeon that the bedroom is "the most important room in the house. He thought you should sit up in bed and feel wonderful." McKeon's bedroom was no exception. It was furnished with a large-scale to-the-ceiling canopy bed, sumptuously draped and dressed in off-white diamond-quilted linen. Taylor favored the subtly textured fabric. He also used it on the pair of his signature catcher's mitt chairs flanking the fireplace in the bedroom's sitting area. The ornate gilt occasional chair, covered in chartreuse silk, and the pair of Giacometti bronze stools alongside the travertine table exemplified Taylor's adeptness at eclecticism.

MRS. STANLEY DOLLAR JR.

SAN FRANCISCO, CALIFORNIA, 1982

Nancy Dollar (Mrs. Stanley), Diana Knowles's sister-in-law, com-missioned Taylor, in collaboration with Porter and Steinwedell, to extensively remodel her Mediterranean-style palazzo in Pacific Heights. The project, which expanded the footprint of the baronial house, took over four years to execute. Although Taylor assembled a rare collection of French, English, and Chinese antiques for Dollar, he died before the job was finished. Suzanne Tucker completed the assignment.

DINING ROOM

Hand-painted eighteenth-century Chinese wall-paper from Frederick P. Victoria & Son and bare antique parquet floors comprised the elegant backdrop in Dollar's dining room, which Taylor furnished with a Directoire walnut dining table and twelve Louis XV provincial green-and-cream painted chairs. The rare eighteenth-century crystal chandelier and the pair of Baccarat candelabra garnishing the table reflected luminously throughout the handsome interior.

LIVING ROOM

Taylor furnished Dollar's living room exquisitely. He outfitted the commodious interior with sev-eral seating areas, underscoring them with an ex-pansive European Savonnerie-style carpet.

The living room's principal vignette was anchored by a Syrie Maugham sofa upholstered in tufted yellow Thai silk. The sofa was radiant, especially against the lustrous backdrop of an eighteenth-century Chinese coromandel lacquer screen depicting exotic flora and fauna and vari-ous objects and still lifes.

The black-and-gilt lacquer low table fronting the sofa was also eighteenth-century Chinese. It coexisted flawlessly with the flanking pairs of Louis XV–style gilt wood bergères and Louis XVI–style ormolu and marble gueridons. The pair of Louis XV–style ormolu-mounted Chinese lavender earthenware candelabra furthered the setting's delectable color palette.

GARDEN ROOM

Taylor purchased from Frederick P. Victoria &
Son, the respected New York antiques dealer, a
suite of seat furniture along with three life-size
tole trees that Jansen of Paris made and sold
to Elsie de Wolfe for her infamous Circus Ball.
The festive ball took place at La Villa Trianon at
Versailles in 1938. Taylor thought the whimsical
furniture, with its twisted tree-trunk motif,
was idyllic for Dollar's completely gutted and
renovated white garden room, and she agreed
wholeheartedly with him.

The suite of furniture, which included a
white-painted metal banquette and pouffe as
well as a conversation piece adorned with a
painted blackamoor figure holding a pair of
umbrellas, provided the garden room with
diverse seating. The towering white-and-green-
painted metal trees, including the extra model
Victoria made for the room, put the finishing
touch on the imaginative setting, which
overlooked the new pretty little private green
courtyard Taylor outlined with a mature privet
hedge to screen it from Vallejo Street.

PRIVATE RESIDENCE

SAN FRANCISCO, CALIFORNIA, 1983

LIVING ROOM

Taylor decorated the living room in this early 1950s contemporary house in accord with his clients' renowned collection of contemporary art. He created an interior of the utmost simplicity and sophistication, ensuring that the backdrop of restrained color and subtle textures complemented, without imposing on, the masterpieces it displayed.

Balance was fundamental to Taylor's successful plan for the living room, which he arranged with two distinct seating areas. The principal seating area, consisting of a flanking pair of overscaled banquettes upholstered in heavy white tufted ribbed cotton, was grouped around a fireplace Taylor shaped on site with a cardboard model of the mantel and box cutters.

Taylor fabricated the contemporary fireplace in black granite, augmenting its classic understated profile with angled legs and roughly chiseled sides. The distinctive texture was also applied to the paired grouping of black-granite triangular coffee tables serving the two banquettes. Although the two tables were equally sized, Taylor differentiated their height by two inches and spaced them five inches apart.

The living room's second seating area was arranged diagonally across from the fireside grouping on the opposite side of the room. It was anchored by a long overscaled backless banquette, also upholstered in heavy white tufted ribbed cotton. Taylor designed one black-granite coffee table for the vignette, detailing it identically to the triangular pair.

The English walnut secretary and the suite of five Italian Empire caned armchairs enhanced the classicism of the interior. Although Taylor was partial to the parcel-gilt and black-painted chair, he only located one of them for the room. Fortunately, he was able to make four copies of the antique chair, replicating it perfectly, down to the lion's head arm terminals and their metal ring mounts.

Taylor arranged the living room chairs strategically, grouping them with the three banquettes. The chairs, while functional to the seating plan, were also an important source of color. Their linen seat cushions disseminated coherent and effective touches of yellow throughout the interior.

MR. GIL GARFIELD

LOS ANGELES, CALIFORNIA, 1983

Gil Garfield valued working with Taylor for the second time when, in 1983, he bought a small stucco pavilion-style house in Los Angeles. Taylor's decoration of Garfield's new home also coincided with another breakthrough in his decorating style. He was spending quality time in the Far East and returned from an eighty-day trip around the world just before starting the second project with Garfield. Taylor adopted minimalism as his latest approach to design, creating interiors for Garfield that were completely Zen.

Garfield's new house, which was designed by John Woolf (1908–1980), the celebrated Los Angeles architect, appealed to Taylor. He liked the glossy squares of black granite covering the floors and the large windows and skylights flooding the interiors with natural light. Taylor capitalized on each of these elements when planning the space.

LIVING ROOM

Taylor decorated Garfield's living room in strict black and off-white. He fabricated the room's tables, pedestals, fireplace mantel, and accessories in black granite, correlating them with the dramatic floors. The bamboo window blinds that screened the windows and doors overlooking the swimming pool with its creamy white limestone terrace were also stained black.

Contrast, texture, and geometric shapes excelled in the living room. The two overscaled V-shaped sofas, upholstered in a burlap-weave terra-cotta-tinted off-white silk, were designed to fit, puzzle-like, with the hexagonal coffee table displaying a Roman fragment from Garfield's notable collection of antiquities. The live banyan tree, the fossilized-like stone lighting fixtures displayed on the granite pedestals, and Taylor's manipulation of natural light completed the understated feeling of the room.

DINING ROOM

The juxtaposition of the classical Roman fragment with contemporary art comprised the
natural transition between the house's living
room and its dining room. Taylor furnished the
intimate dining room, which opened onto the
pool terrace, with a round black-granite dining
table and Philippine rattan chairs he designed,
lacquered black and cushioned and upholstered
in burlap-weave terra-cotta-tinted off-white silk.

MR. AND MRS. GORHAM B. KNOWLES

LAKE TAHOE, CALIFORNIA, 1983

Gorham and Diana Knowles, who had spent summers with their respective families at Lake Tahoe since early childhood, purchased their contemporary redwood and glass house and its private four-hundred-foot cove on the California side of the lake during the early 1980s. They named the hillside retreat steeped in firs and pines Tamarack Cove after Tamarack, Diana's 1930 wood-hull Garwood speedboat given to her when she was very young by her father, Stanley Dollar. The Tahoe house, which was Taylor's fourth commission for the Knowleses, coincided with his work on the Presidio Heights house. It also followed the early 1970s assignment he did for them at their weekend house in Pebble Beach, California.

LIVING ROOM

Taylor kept comfort and the region's superlative natural setting equally in mind when he planned the Knowleses' Tahoe living room. He mixed luxuriously upholstered overscaled furniture with distinctive organic elements, creating one of the pinnacle interiors of his career.

The living room's principal seating area, anchored by a Taylor-designed L-shaped sofa nestled into a corner of the room and covered in off-white hand-woven chenille, was oriented toward the two-story wall of glass overlooking the cove. White ball and celery-green pillows, also in chenille, accented the sofa, which underscored a Charles Arnoldi tree-branch sculpture and a pair of nineteenth-century Austrian metal-and-horn deer heads hanging on walls of bleached cedar siding.

The raw rock table fronting the sofa had exceptional presence. Although the twenty-eight-hundred-pound table was Taylor's housewarming gift to the Knowleses "because they were good clients" of his, the largesse did not include its time-consuming delivery and complicated installation requiring a sizable crane, a foreman, and a crew of eight men. However, that was only part of the costly and arduous task. Taylor, without consulting the Knowleses, instructed their contractor to reinforce the floor of the living room and its new adjacent redwood deck in order to accommodate the overwhelming weight of the rock.

Taylor's "lovely gift" to the Knowleses cost them over ten thousand "lovely" dollars. It also "scared Diana to death" when the enormous rock, which was craned from the front of the house to the back deck, started bouncing three inches from the peak of the house's roof as it was maneuvered downward. "She realized that one false move could have taken the whole house right down the hill and into the lake." Although the house quaked when the rock landed on the deck, Knowles had already "fled to Tahoe City until it was safely installed" in the living room.

LIBRARY

The Knowleses' library, which extended off the living room and also overlooked the cove, was decorated in rich earth tones. Cinnamon chenille covered the room's pair of catchers' mitt chairs while white ribbed cotton distinguished the principal seating area's tufted banquette and ash-framed log-and-rush Douglas armchair.

Organic elements were also crucial in the library. Although the native stone paving the fireplace wall preexisted Taylor's decoration of the room, he added several of his favored stone mill wheels to the decor. He propped one wheel on the fireplace hearth and used a pair of them as tops for the custom-made occasional tables fronting the banquette. Fortunately, Taylor didn't have to travel further than his warehouse in order to locate the three mill wheels. He bought and stored every one of them he found, replicating the stone model in plastic when the horde dwindled.

DINING ROOM

Taylor decorated the Knowleses' dining room simply, deferring to its all-encompassing backdrop of Tamarack Cove and Lake Tahoe beyond. He also planned the interior for informal family-style meals, outfitting its custom-designed round ash dining table with a lazy Susan and twelve "Buffalo-Bill" bleached ash and rush-seat chairs. The dining room's deer-horn chandelier and pair of eighteenth-century Japanese wood deer were part and parcel of the elegant wilderness characterizing Tamarack Cove.

MR. AND MRS. ALLAN SIMON

RANCHO SANTA FE, CALIFORNIA, 1983

GREAT ROOM

The great room was the center of Allan and Stefani Simons' hacienda-style ranch house that Cliff May (1908–1989)—the notable architect who pioneered the California ranch-style house—designed in 1974 for another couple. Although Taylor respected May's work, he lightened the interior of the house from its original dark incarnation. He bleached the majority of the woodwork, including the beams that spanned the high-pitched grape-stake ceiling in the great room.

Taylor also instilled the great room with a relaxed casualness. He anchored the airy interior with a capacious two-piece sectional and an over-scaled coffee table in bleached oak with a fossilized stone top. A pair of ottomans, also in bleached oak and cushioned in colorful striped serapes that were found on the Simons' property, completed the great room's principal sitting area.

GREAT ROOM CLOSEUP

Taylor perpetuated the lessons he had learned from Rudolph Schaeffer throughout his entire career. In the great room, the hot Mexican colors of blue, green, pink, and lemon yellow radiated against the backdrop of the warm clay-white walls, the patterned rug, and the Kravet white ribbed cotton upholstery. Taylor also valued the great room's synchronized relationship with the outdoors through its elongated skylight and the expansive contiguous central courtyard.

DINING AREA

Oversized banana plants created a natural division between the great room's living and dining areas, without diminishing the openness of its forty-three-foot-long expanse. Natural light poured into the dining area through the ceiling's skylight, illuminating the pair of Mexican wooden dining tables and the accompanying natural-colored *equipales* chairs.

Taylor's assignment for Allan and Stefani Simon is long remembered and highly valued. Benjamin Simon, the Simons' son, who is an architectural designer today, recalls that "having had the privilege of spending time with Michael Taylor during his work on my parents' former home by Cliff May in Rancho Santa Fe, I was taken back to that time of witnessing his true design genius and innovation. . . . If I was able to absorb only a small percentage of Taylor's vast gifts through inspiration, I count that as a blessing and much more than sufficient."

MR. AND MRS. RICHARD CRAMER

INDIAN WELLS, CALIFORNIA, 1984

Taylor's assignment for Richard and Alice Cramer was formidable. It involved transforming the well-located but unremarkable early 1970s one-story vacation house they had recently purchased at a private golf club into an imposing California contemporary design. The footprint of the original house was expanded, ceilings and rooflines were raised, and the view from the house was oriented toward the garden, swimming pool, and neighboring mountains through newly installed walls of tinted glass.

The new white Italian travertine floors throughout the interior's open floor plan and also extending outside to the pool area and surrounding terraces created boundless parameters characteristic of Taylor's work. In fact, when he completed the Indian Wells job, nothing remained of the original structure.

MORNING ROOM

Taylor furnished the morning room against new walls of glass screened identically to his own dining room and the Wilson pool pavilion. The pierced wooden grille work, which was equally striking in the Cramer house, projected a restrained pattern and texture into the colorless grouping of seating upholstered in off-white basket-weave silk.

LIVING ROOM
TOWARD PIANO

The commodious living room, with its open floor plan and off-white color scheme, was composed of several seating areas. The principal seating was arranged in the center of the room, aligning its generous grouping of furniture with a full-length span of exposed glass overlooking the garden courtyard. The backdrop of the outdoors, the flourishing leaves of the surrounding Ficus Benjamina trees, and the apricot basket-weave silk cushions and pillows enhanced the setting without imposing on its restfulness. The skylit bank of trees edging the piano separated the living room from the dining room.

DINING ROOM

Taylor increased the source of natural light in the dining room. He incorporated another division of skylights along the length of the built-in credenza, underscoring the room's predominant wall of whitewashed brick and the flanking arrangements of white Miltonia orchids. The travertine dining table and the woven-leather Budji chairs sustained the principal elements that were consistently infused throughout the interior of the house.

MASTER BEDROOM

Taylor decorated the Cramers' master bedroom in one of his favorite fabrics: Lee Jofa's multicolored Jardin Chinois Handprint. The lightly glazed cotton fabric, liberally quilted and depicting birds of paradise within an exotic floral setting, diffused pastel shades of blue, yellow, peach, and green throughout the pristinely white bedroom. The French stone fireplace mantel and the sandblasted and bleached-oak grille work screening the windows contributed rusticity and texture to the eminently appealing interior.

MR. AND MRS. JOHN G. BOWES

SAN FRANCISCO, CALIFORNIA, 1985

LIVING ROOM TOWARD BAY

The townhouse's living room, dining room, and library were located on the piano nobile. Taylor unified the three rooms by paving their floors in polished black slate. He also specified white walls as the appropriate backdrop for the Bowes's significant collection of contemporary art. Taylor, Walker, and the Boweses' gave special attention to the bayside elevation in the living room. Taylor wanted to bracket the expansive view. He insisted on softening the floor-to-ceiling wall of glass with foot-wide wooden pillars. Although Walker suggested six-inch-wide pillars, he and Taylor deferred to John Bowes's judgment. They opted for nine-inch-wide pillars, which segmented the glass into four equal sections of four feet.

LIVING ROOM

The fireplace's black-granite wall governed Taylor's symmetrical arrangement of the furniture in the living room. He placed a sofa of his own design on the wall directly opposite the fireplace. The sofa, which was upholstered in white crowder chenille and skirted with bouillon fringe, offset a pair of polished black-granite end tables. The flanking pair of Louis XV–style armchairs from the archbishop's palace in Turin and the low Chinese lacquered coffee table infused eclecticism into the setting. The second seating area was composed of a balanced pair of banquettes and polished black-granite demilune sofa tables, which sat perpendicular to the fireplace wall. The banquettes, also upholstered in white chenille, increased the seating capacity of the room without diminishing its circulation. This was important, as it was necessary to pass through the living room in order to reach the library, which formed an L at the bayside end of the living room.

LIVING ROOM TOWARD FIREPLACE

Taylor also treated the fireplace wall innovatively. At first he "had this idea of a black lacquer screen over the mantel," but instead, he told the Boweses, "We'll do it out of black granite." He held up black plastic bags against the wall to convince them that they would like it. The end result was a floor-to-ceiling massing of polished black granite that simulated a six-panel screen. The panels looked folded, with their edges concealed by mitered seams. The firebox was recessed and centered at the base of the stone screen.

DINING ROOM

The Boweses' dining room was situated at the fore of the living room, behind a pair of 1920s floor-to-ceiling doors painted by Armand-Albert Rateau. Rateau was a French decorator and architect who was a proponent of Art Deco. The rosewood dining table and the accompanying suite of twelve chairs, made by Eugene Printz, the noted French cabinetmaker, were also chic.

8 "looked at the beauty of shells, tree stumps, rocks, and flowers—into the beauty of things that cost nothing". Russell MacMaster's eulogy for Michael Taylor, June 5, 1986.

8 "was in the forefront of art education in the perception and use of colors". *San Francisco Chronicle*, March 10, 1988, Sec. B, p.7.

8 "opened my eyes to vistas I wasn't aware of. He made me conscious of possibilities". Lois Wagner Green, "California's Golden Boy of Décor," *California Living*, XXIX (1983), 10.

8 "the secrets of color". *San Francisco Chronicle*, March 10, 1988, Sec. B, p.7.

8 "the most efficient color for capturing both natural and man-made light". Suzanne Trocmé, "Michael Taylor. His Brilliant Use of Scale and Light Announced the California Look," *Architectural Digest*, LVII (2000), 252.

8 "his dear Michael". Letter from Rudolph Schaeffer to Michael Taylor, August 26, 1983.

8 "wild, but extremely creative". Ibid.

8 "fireworks" that were "going off all the time". Ibid.

8 "she certainly was one of the guiding forces in the whole development of what is the American style today". Dupuy Warrick Reed, "A New American Style," *Connoisseur*, CCXIV (1984), 86.

10 "a new look in furniture". "A New Look In Furniture," *House Beautiful*, XCV (1953), 190.

10 "the new, rich look now entering our homes". Ibid.

10 "graceful merging of design influence". Ibid. p.4.

10 they shared the same clientele. Interview with Byron Meyer, October 7, 2005.

11 plants prevent "a room from feeling over-decorated". Katharine Tweed, *The Finest Rooms by America's Great Decorators* (New York. The Viking Press, 1964), p.158.

11 "soften the light". Ibid.

11 "help a room breathe and feel alive". *San Francisco Examiner*, November 19, 1974. p.24.

11 "the plant in a basket craze". Interview with Chuck Williams, October 31, 2005.

11 "fresh way to keep a white bedroom fresh". "Fresh way to keep a white bedroom fresh," *Vogue*, CXXVIII (1956), 268.

11 "advocated a strong secondary color, and repetitive use of printed fabrics for 'a certain purity' and a bold and unified effect". "Timeless Rooms," *House & Garden*, CLXV (1993), 188.

11 "there is a tremendous amount of color in my rooms, but there are not many colors". Ibid.

12 "never forgot beautiful things. He constantly absorbed everything he saw and banked it, to be a source of reference". Lois Wagner Green, "California's Golden Boy of Décor," *California Living*, XXIX (1983), 15.

12 "it's got to sing and talk back to you, and be A plus, plus if it crosses the threshold" of your house. Interview with Candy Hamm, February 16, 2006.

12 "Nini Martin came in and bought it, lock, stock and barrel, for her oldest daughter". Lois Wagner Green, "California's Golden Boy of Décor," *California Living*, XXIX (1983), 12.

12 "lively, fresh, and very different". Interview with Dorothea Walker, January 23, 1998.

12 "Madison Avenue's slick magazines" were always asking "What's new of Michael's work? His rooms, full of flowers and light, sold more copies for them than any designer in the world". Russell MacMaster's eulogy for Michael Taylor, June 5, 1986.

13 "He worked terribly, terribly hard. In the midst of a party, he'd sit down and work on sketches". *San Francisco Chronicle*, February 8, 1980, p.26.

13 "to get his clients totally immersed and passionate about their collaboration with him". Interview with Gil Garfield, February 4, 2006.

13 He wanted them to react and commit to what he was proposing for them. Interview with Coby Everdell, February 3, 2006.

14 "illuminating him to handsome, intimidating advantage". e mail from John Crocker, September 20, 2007.

14 "a relentless interrogation". Interview with Douglas S. Cramer, September 28, 2005.

14 "on seeing the completed room, Walker remarked to Taylor that it reminded her of the Chambre d'Amour at Biarritz or the Costa Brava and joked that all it needed was a little sand.". Interview with Dorothea Walker, January 23, 1998.

16 "Two Mikes in Her Life". *San Francisco Examiner*, October 8, 1961.

16 "the great white plague". Interview with Jeanne Jackson, August 25, 2005.

16 "Do those knots make you nervous?". Ibid.

16 "Isn't that chic? It must be from Michael Taylor!". Interview with Delores Dana, June 30, 2006.

16 "the Golden Boy". Interview with Elaine McKeon, January 16, 2006.

16 "to do something about Maryon's clothes". Interview with Maryon Davies Lewis, July 3, 2006.

16 "very close to our work". Lois Wagner Green, "California's Golden Boy of Décor," *California Living*, XXIX (1983), 12.

18 "made up the final chapter in Tweed's extraordinary book, heralding him as the rising star of the younger generation". Letter from Albert Hadley, July 10, 2007.

18 "He had no regard for money as long as it wasn't his". Interview with Stanley Beyer, March 18, 2006.

18 "get some more and call me when you have it!". Interview with Fred and Nina Carroll, January 18, 2006.

18 "he'd go ahead and do it anyways". Interview with Fred Lyon, January 21, 2005.

19 "he had a very good time doing it," and "loved what [Taylor] did". Interview with Rene Gregorius, April 15, 2007.

19 "When you take things out, you must increase the size of what's left". Lars Lerup, "A Natural Touch," *Architectural Digest*, XLII (1985), 34.

19 "I think we should get rid of those tassels". Interview with Dodie Rosekrans, January 20, 2006.

19 "If I ever do another house, I'll have him". Interview with Diana Knowles, January 26, 2005.

19 "a jewel box". Ibid.

19 "hydraneas". Interview with Fred Lyon, January 21, 2005.

19 "the most gorgeous restrooms in San Francisco". Interview with Lynn Bergeron, December 1, 2005.

20 "that people loved to look at themselves". Interview with Ardath Rouas, February 20, 2006.

20 "I've done all I can do." He then added, "I hope the food is good". Interview with Claude Rouas, January 14, 2006.

20 "didn't want simple". Interview with Ardath Rouas, February 20, 2006.

20 "Have you already signed the lease? I can't do anything with this dump!". Ibid.

20 "important tool". Interview with Claude Rouas, January 14, 2006.

21 "opened the gate, walked through the garden, opened the front door and looked right through into the Pacific Ocean, crashing onto the rocks below". Lois Wagner Green, "California's Golden Boy of Décor," *California Living*, XXIX (1983), 12.

21 "pitched right in and paid their bills". Ibid.

21 "when in doubt, throw it out". Dorothea Walker". Taylor-Made," *House & Garden*, CLXIII (1991), 172.

21 "design the interior in any formal sense." He "just moved everything in". Sam Burchell, "The Collectors. Michael Taylor in San Francisco," *Architectural Digest*, XXXIV (1977), 14.

21 "You really want to photograph it, do you?". *The Estate of Michael Taylor*, p.8.

21 an "apocalypse". Interview with Melanie Fleischmann, September 26, 2006.

21 "like walking through the looking glass". Interview with Russell Mac-Masters, September 1, 2006.

21 "more surreal than, over and beyond anything you'd anticipate finding in any of his clients' homes. It was him". Ibid.

37 "sculpture in rooms and gardens". "New Shop Talk—Los Angeles, Paris," *House & Garden*, CXLVII (1975), 6.

37 "a very rare cactus that only grows in two places in the world". Ibid.

38 "You can only have one architect, John Lautner". Interview with Lynn Beyer, January 29, 2006.

38 He "wanted to suit in every way this rocky point and create a durable, sheltered, livable outlook to the panorama of rocks, coves, beach, and ocean". Elizabeth McMillian and Melba Levick, *Beach Houses from Malibu to Laguna* (New York. Rizzioli, 1994), p.20.

38 "a large free-flowing space with a high sloping ceiling and window walls, a kind of observation deck". Jesse Kornbluth, "Pacific Overtone," *Architectural Digest*, XLII (1985), 151.

38 "among the best he's ever done". Ibid.

38 "whose acumen was matched only by their stamina and taste". Ibid, p.146.

38 'wanted a place that was visually exciting,' and 'where the climate was good'. Louise Bernikow, "La Quinta Norte. Douglas S. Cramer's Ranch in the Santa Ynez Valley ," *Architectural Digest*, XLIV (1987), 137-138.

39 "the preeminent California designer". Ibid, p.138.

39 "was very special, and had the magic touch". Interview with Denise Hale, September 30, 2005.

39 "loved the project". Interview with Douglas S. Cramer, September 28, 2005.

39 "a papal blessing". Ibid.

39 "confronted the entire building process, leading Choate and Cramer onto his concept of one large two story house". e-mail from Douglas S. Cramer, October 7, 2005.

39 "one towering armada". Interview with Douglas S. Cramer, September 28, 2005.

39 "Taylor waved his magic wand," insisting the foundation "be moved three feet backwards from the road for a better view". Ibid.

39 "a force of nature you can't tackle". Ibid.

39 "insane perfectionism". Idib.

39 "Nothing took too much time, no quest for the right object would be cut short—whatever it took, the house would be exactly as they [Cramer and Taylor] dreamed it". Louise Bernikow, "La Quinta Norte. Douglas S. Cramer's Ranch in the Santa Ynez Valley," *Architectural Digest*, XLIV (1987), 138-139.

39 "he was so ingrained with the look and feel of the house". Interview with Douglas S. Cramer, September 28, 2005.

39 "live and enjoy his art". Ibid.

39 "had a fit". Ibid.

39 "allowed". Interview with Douglas S. Cramer, September 28, 2005.

39 "to show off the room better". Ibid.

39 "And why not? Kelly will never know the difference!". Ibid.

39 "asked for a chair that was 'free and pillowy' but would not compete with the Simons' vast art collection". *San Francisco Chronicle*, February 8, 1980, p.26.

39 "big enough to lie down on or curl up in". Ibid.

40 "veiled women from the gaze of men". Nermine Abdel Gelil, "A New Mashrabiyya for Contemporary Cairo. Integrating Traditional Latticework from Islamic and Japanese Cultures," *Journal of Asian Architecture and Building Engineering*, V (2006), 37.

41 "You are my brother!". Interview with Dede Wilsey, January 12, 2006.

41 "their guests to feel like they were south of somewhere—not a specific place, but a feeling reminiscent of a romantic place in the sun where they might have traveled to, yet completely at home where it was". Interview with Ardath Rouas, February 20, 2006.

41 "on a big rock, shaded by a circle of olive trees". Bruce David Colen, "Napa Valley's Auberge du Soleil. A Touch of Provence in Northern California," *Architectural Digest*, XLIII (1986), 118.

41 "a wonderful book of drawings of different kinds of French country architecture". Interview with Ardath Rouas, February 20, 2006.

41 "everyone agreed that it changed the whole ambiance of the entrance". Ibid.

42 "created as he went along. Each time he came [to the Auberge], there were changes". Interview with Claude Rouas, January 14, 2006.

46 "the ultimate consumer" He had "very definite ideas of what a hotel room should be". Interview with Ardath Rouas, February 20, 2006.

46 'Okay, here I am, your first guest, eager for a week of luxurious relaxation. Where do I go and what do I do next? Every step and every hour of the way has to be gracious serendipity, or I may not come back again'. Bruce David Colen, "Napa Valley's Auberge du Soleil. A Touch of Provence in Northern California," *Architectural Digest*, XLIII (1986), 200.

46 "wanted to eliminate the sense that another person had used the room before". Ibid, p.122.

46 "Taylor to control the day-to-day look without operational interpretation". e-mail from Adair Borba, April 6, 2007.

48 "expected his vision to be executed exactly". Interview with Adair Borba, March 1, 2006.

48 "beautifully casual, but not haphazardly placed". Ibid.

48 "a great feel". Interview with Ned Spieker, February 21, 2006.

48 "carry over". Ibid.

49 "it just won't do that the elevators and the lobby don't match the halls". Ibid.

49 "audacious and unabashed". Ibid.

49 "it will sparkle and be a beautiful building". Ibid.

49 "lots of buildings". Ibid.

50 "the biggest slip-covering of his career!". Ibid.

50 "one hell of a house". Interview with Dodie Rosekrans, January 20, 2006.

50 "she had spoken to God today?". Ibid.

50 "outrageous in a way, yet absolutely correct and classical in his work. His taste was infallible and incredible. If he had lived," she said, "he'd have been more wonderful than ever". Ibid.

50 "I don't want a typical Michael Taylor house". Linda Bucklin, "In the Light of the Bay," *House & Garden*, CLIX (1987), 126.

50 "and what exactly is that?". Ibid.

50 "Oh you know, white on white, wicker everywhere, huge overstuffed chairs. My feet don't reach the floor. I feel like a pygmy". Ibid.

50 "what?". Interview with Dede Wilsey, January 12, 2006.

50 "well good God, I'm going to make you a Michael Taylor sofa. You'll have to get up and sit somewhere else!". Ibid.

50 "What are you doing?". Ibid.

50 We're decorating". Ibid.

50 "From where?". Ibid.

50 "but once he saw it, he took full credit". Ibid.

50 "came up over dinner at Russell MacMaster's house". e-mail from Paul Weaver, April 30, 2007.

51 "sole and separate from Taylor's design business". "Memorandum of Understanding" between Michael Taylor and Paul Weaver, August 1, 1985, p.1.

51 "to honor outstanding designers working in the field". Interview with Lester Dundes, December 1985.

51 "great fun together". Interview with Diana Knowles, January 26, 2005.

51 "After working so often together, Michael Taylor and Diana had an idyllic, almost rhapsodic friendship". Dorothea Walker, "Gorham Knowles House," unpublished article.

51 "you can talk to me all night and I'm not going to change my mind. I know what I like and what I don't like". Interview with Diana Knowles, January 26, 2005.

51 "graceful and charming". Dorothea Walker, "Gorham Knowles House," unpublished article.

51 "They had been looking for a larger house for several years". Ibid.

51 "envisioned a new-old palace rising". Ibid.

51 "garish" chintz". Ibid.

51 "a broad spectrum of individuals whose life had been touched by him—the Hollywood elite, wealthy clients, benefactors, as well as members of the trade". e-mail from David Burkholder, June 21, 2007.

51 "very beautiful people, predominately male". e-mail from Douglas S. Cramer, June 21, 2007.

51 "The silence was deafening as he approached the podium". e-mail from Russell MacMasters, June 28, 2007.

51 "precisely stitched together with red roses". e-mail from Paul Weaver, August 29, 2007.

51 "We were the lucky ones who knew Michael and could experience the thrill of divine inspiration, of genius. . . . We also experienced first-hand his exhilarating creative energy . . . a force that reached around the globe in his lifetime and that will long continue to inspire creative people everywhere". Russell MacMaster's eulogy for Michael Taylor, June 5, 1986.

51 "Genius is not always compassionate. To resist Michael's creative power was taking on Goliath". Ibid.

51 He "was tough . . . a difficult friend" and "relentlessly critical of the mundane, of the cliché, intolerant of the mediocre, and yet, devastatingly self-effacing and funny". Ibid.

51 He "could talk like Baby Snooks and make me laugh so hard, I cried, and yet, inspire me to work harder than I ever thought possible. The rewards of sharing his great sensitivity and wit have been stunning gifts for us all". Ibid.

51 "Michael changed the way we lived. He blasted through the reverence and formality so prevalent in design years ago and brought nature indoors". *The New York Times*, June 5, 1986, Sec. B, p. 16.

52 He "made decorating history. Whatever he did, or didn't do, made news". *The Estate of Michael Taylor*, p.8.

52 "had soured in recent years". *San Francisco Examiner*, December 26, 1988, Sec.B, p.7.

52 "she wouldn't consider hiring anyone else". *San Francisco Examiner*, March 19, 1987, Sec. F, p.4.

52 "heard of his death," she was "having everything in the bedroom copied as a living tribute to Michael." She planned "to live happily in that white monotone bedroom for another twenty-two years". Ibid.

52 "The room had a real energy and buzz, more like a big party than an auction. There was scarcely a decorator of any note from California, southern or northern, who wasn't there, and more than a few from the East Coast". e-mail from Douglas S. Cramer, May 16, 2006.

53 "rapier-sharp tailfins". David Welch and Gerry Khermouch, "Can GM Save an Icon?," *Business Week*, 3777 (2002), 60.

53 When he dressed in one of his characteristic ways, with his shirtsleeves rolled up, there was often a watch on each wrist. Interview with Bob Miller, March 20, 2006.

53 "the James Dean of decorators". Suzanne Trocmé, "Michael Taylor. His Brilliant Use of Scale and Light Announced the California Look," *Architectural Digest*, LVII (2000), 229.

53 "the innovative one. An original". Pilar Viladas, "Taylor-Made," *House & Garden*, CLXIII (1991), 107.

53 "bleeders, followers, and leeches". *San Francisco Chronicle*, February 8, 1980, p.26.

54 She "spotted" his talent. Interview with Nancy Kibbey, May 7, 2006.

54 "that his approach would be fresh, exuberant and natural". Howard Junker, "Test of Time. Designer's Debut Presages a California Style," *Architectural Digest*, XLI (1984), 46.

54 "Mrs. Turner's immaculate style" and "the architectural detailing of Mr. Wurster". Ibid.

54 'smuggled' "in from Florida, airfreighted in a carpet packing tube". Ibid.

59 he wasn't able to persuade her. Interview with Wade Bentson, January 16, 2006.

60 the shapes of the banquettes for her drawing room with string outlines on the [office] floor. Brooke Hayward, "Thomas and Nan Kempner in New York. Evolution of a Park Avenue Apartment," *Architectural Digest*, XLIV (1987), 170.

60 reminded her of a bordello—not a salon!. Ibid.

60 'every decorator in town tried to come in and knock it off'. Ibid, p. 17.

60 "hoisted through the [Kempner's] window". Ibid, p. 170.

63 "which depicted birds and butterflies flitting in and out of grafted trees tied with ribbons". Chippy Irvine and Alex McLean, *Private New York. Remarkable Residences* (New York. Abbeville Press, 1990), p.172.

63 influenced by one of Dodie Rosekrans's long coral necklaces. *Los Angeles Times*, October 13, 1976, Sec. F, p.2.

64 'so there was no need to change the arrangement,' or the furniture. "Keeping The Best, Updating The Rest," *House & Garden*, CXLVI (1974), 85.

64 "color and pattern". Ibid.

64 Taylor's use of "warm whites spiked with yellow," related the living room to "its garden vista". Faber Birren, "Color comes first," *House & Garden*, CXII (1957), 64.

64 "how to make a room more inviting by keeping the best, updating the rest". "Keeping The Best, Updating The Rest," *House & Garden*, CXLVI (1974), 83.

64 "one touch of today could be all you need to give your favorite room a lift". Ibid.

68 "stop by". Interview with Peggy Richards, August 22, 2006.

68 "besides herself". Ibid.

68 "that she dropped her dolly". Ibid.

72 "The bedroom, too long a bare chamber, is getting a new graceful dress inspired by fashion's Empire Look". "The Country Look," *House & Garden*, CXV (1959), 38.

72 "this grand tradition". Ibid.

73 "on the principle that if each thing is beautiful in itself, its period is irrelevant". "A Personal Hobby can set the theme for a weekend house," *House & Garden*, CXVI (1959), 76.

76 "always fantasized that you lived outdoors in your house". Interview with Russell MacMasters, January 15, 2006.

81 "live like a bachelor". Interview with Maryon Davies Lewis, October 3, 2005.

83 "the lady had too long a skirt". Ibid.

83 "onto a rectangular steel frame, covering completely the curved steel arms and the straight posts at the corners of the bed that supported it". "Surprise is the Theme," *House & Garden*, CXXXI (1967), 164.

83 "just who do you think you are?". Interview with Maryon Davies Lewis, October 3, 2005.

83 "When I finish this house, Maryon, I want you to be able to grow old here". Ibid.

84 "horrified". Interview with Maryon Davies Lewis, October 3, 2005.

100 "that a horse would feel comfortable in". Interview with Jeanne Jackson, January 19, 2006.

100 the anthracite shag rug be impenetrable to cigarette ashes. Interview with Wade Bentson, January 16, 2006.

102 "nondescript boxlike". "Decorating in a New Mood," *House & Garden*, CXXIX (1966), 85.

102 did his best work in front of the camera. Interview with Fred Lyon, January 21, 2005.

104 "In ten years, you've never bought a good piece of furniture?". Interview with Lynn Beyer, January 29, 2006.

104 "were worthwhile and he had to have them". Ibid.

104 "get rid of the other chairs". Ibid.

107 "Enchanted Cottage" look. Ibid.

107 "on target". Ibid.

110 "fabulous taste". e-mail from Lynn Beyer, July 26, 2007.

110 "Michael was sensational!". Ibid.

127 "Dorothy Fay painstakingly trained that tiny sapling until it grew through the opening to shade the table". e-mail from Fred Lyon, July 31, 2007.

130 like living in a treehouse". "Five Stories of Sunlight," *House & Garden*, CXXXVIII (1970), 112.

147 were unable to free themselves. Interview with Frances Bowes, March 3, 2006.

147 "Oh yes he is". Ibid

147 "Taylor made everything so much fun". Ibid.

147 enhancing the value of their homes. Interview with Bob and Jan MacDonnell, August 28, 2006.

148 "going to tell me [Candy] what to do". Interview with Candy Hamm, February 16, 2006.

150 "invited one to curl up and read a book". Ibid, January 10, 2008.

150 "a catastrophe ensued". Interview with Dorothea Walker, January 23, 1998.

150 "always landed on his feet". Dorothea Walker, "Taylor-Made," *House & Garden*, CLXIII (1991), 113.

157 "every morning when you wake up, I want you to thank me for the furniture, objects and porcelains you bought in London and Paris. It

164 really isn't out there any more". Interview with Candy Hamm, January 10, 2008.

164 "Taylor was so good at things like that". Interview with Elaine McKeon, August 8, 2005.

166 "the most comfortable room he ever designed". Ibid.

174 "find a proper retail space for him". Interview with Byron Meyer, October 7, 2005.

174 "cut-pile carpet, fussy detail and heavy velvet draperies". Diane Dorrans Saeks and John Vaughan, *San Francisco. A Certain Style*, (San Francisco. Chronicle Books, 1989), p. 93.

174 "a poor look" for the interior since the economy was bad at the time. He said "no one will ever know its raw silk". Interview with Byron Meyer, January 4, 2006.

174 "to make everything in the room bigger". Ibid.

188 "I know a lot of Michaels, Michael who?". Interview with Gil Garfield, February 4, 2006.

188 "This is Michael Taylor". Ibid.

188 "lived the rooms". Ibid.

188 He "knew what the key elements had to be by being in the space". Ibid.

194 "something purely American". "Country Modern," *House & Garden*, CL (1978), 99.

194 "Country Modern". Ibid, pp. 96-97.

196 he would not have changed anything. Interview with Dede Wilsey, June 11, 2007.

198 "We'll paint the walls white and visit my friend Nick Wilder". Interview with Liz Familian, January 29, 2006.

209 "bring them up here because they handle the mirrors well". Interview with Alex Phillips, January 14, 2006.

234 "created timelessness in the interiors". Interview with Douglas S. Cramer, September 28, 2005.

242 "when you get to furnishing your apartment, you must have Michael Taylor take a look at it". Interview with Charles Evans, March 6, 2006.

242 Evans "didn't know who he was". Ibid.

242 "putting his thumb up in the air". Ibid.

242 "had a few ideas," and asked him "if he could come up now?". Ibid.

242 "couldn't believe it." Taylor "had furnished the living room". Ibid.

242 "You've got a job". Ibid.

242 "give it to another decorator that very day". Ibid.

245 "just as he had done the mock-up". Ibid.

245 'that all the Parisian fashion salons were done in'. *New York Times*, March 20, 1980, Sec. C, p.8.

251 "impressive" gallery. Dorothea Walker, "Gorham Knowles House," unpublished article.

251 "have a sitting area" in the first floor space. Ibid.

253 "repaired, restored and extended". Ibid.

254 "incensed" at the architects' plan to "enclose the front garden behind a twenty-foot wall". Ibid.

254 "had another brilliant idea". Ibid.

254 "saw her guests playing bridge in the hall". Ibid.

254 "everyone milling around". Ibid.

258 "everything I have here is Michael Taylor. It looks just as good today as the day I bought it". Interview with Diana Knowles, August 31, 2006.

268 "We have to get those trees for Spieker's apartment; their leaves match the acid green of the taffeta stripe pillows". Interview with Tim Marks, January 19, 2006.

272 "old secrets for furniture arranging". Patricia Corbin, "Notes to Help you Decorate-it-Yourself," *House & Garden*, CXLI (1972), 8.

272 "a great spiel". Interview with Dede Wilsey, January 12, 2006.

280 "the most important room in the house. He thought you should sit up in bed and feel wonderful". Diane Dorrans Saeks and John Vaughan, *San Francisco. A Certain Style*, (San Francisco. Chronicle Books, 1989), p. 100.

294 "because they were good clients". Interview with Diana Knowles, August 31, 2006.

294 "scared Diana to death". Interview with Dorothea Walker, January 23, 198.

294 "She realized that one false move could have taken the whole house right down the hill and into the lake". Ibid.

294 "fled to Tahoe City until it was safely installed". Pilar Viladas, "Taylor-Made," *House & Garden*, CLXIII (1998), 172.

300 "having had the privilege of spending time with Michael Taylor during his work on my parents' former home by Cliff May in Rancho Santa Fe, I was taken back to that time of witnessing his true design genius and innovation. . . . .If I was able to absorb only a small percentage of Taylor's vast gifts through inspiration, I count that as a blessing and much more than sufficient". Benjamin Simon (letter to the editor), "Blessing is Taylor-Made," *Architectural Digest*, LXV (2008), 48.

311 "had this idea of a black lacquer screen over the mantel". Interview with Frances Bowes, April 20, 2006.

311 "we'll do it out of black granite". Ibid.

ACKNOWLEDGMENTS

Michael Taylor. Interior Design follows in the footsteps of my passionate and lifelong connection to the brilliant accomplishments of David Adler, the great house architect, and his sister Frances Elkins, the innovative and revolutionary interior designer who greatly influenced Taylor. I first became aware of Adler's work during my freshman year at Lake Forest College in Lake Forest, Illinois, thirty-five years ago. I was intuitively attracted to an eclectic collection of classical houses neighboring the college, not learning until my senior year that Adler had designed all of them. It was then that I asked Franz Schulze, the noted art and architectural historian and one of my college professors, to advise and mentor me for the independent study I wanted to conduct on Adler before graduating. Schulze agreed to my proposal, and when I completed the study four months later he encouraged me to write a book on Adler.

With Schulze's encouragement, which continues to this day, I began to seek a publisher for a book or an article on Adler. In 1980, Architectural Digest commissioned me to write an article on Elkins (Architectural Digest's first "Historic Interiors" feature, in their July–August 1980 issue), the interiors to be those of the Reed house in Lake Forest—the pinnacle collaboration between the brother and sister. That assignment, and a second article about Elkins's interiors executed in Adler houses, which appeared in Architectural Digest's January 2000 issue, gave me the opportunity to learn more about Elkins. The articles were also the precursors to The Country Houses of David Adler (2001) and Frances Elkins. Interior Design (2005), two books that I have written for W. W. Norton & Company.

The idea for Michael Taylor. Interior Design emerged just as Frances Elkins. Interior Design was going to print. It was January 2005, and I was preparing for a trip to Los Angeles. Two days before leaving for the West Coast, I had a premonition that my next book would be about Michael Taylor. However, it wasn't until a few days later in Los Angeles when I visited Rose Tarlow, the renowned author and interior designer and my long-standing friend, that the idea jelled in my mind. Tarlow had supported my interest in Adler and Elkins since we first met during the late 1980s at Melrose House, her West Hollywood, California, showroom. She had long admired Adler and Elkins, and we always enjoyed discussing them whenever I visited her. Tarlow wrote one of the book jacket reviews for Frances Elkins. Interior Design (Bill Hodgins also reviewed the book) and generously offered (during the January 2005 visit) to write the foreword to my next book. Although I accepted Tarlow's valued offer, I told her I was unsure of the topic. My indecision changed, however, when she confirmed my momentary instinct and suggested that I write a book about Michael Taylor. I am greatly honored that Rose wrote the foreword to this book.

Fortunately, my exposure to Michael Taylor and his work developed as I researched Adler and Elkins. Although I was already familiar with Taylor's work through House & Garden and Architectural Digest, it was because of my introduction to the late Dorothea Walker, the longtime West Coast contributing editor to House & Garden and Vogue, that I learned firsthand about him. Katherine Boyd (Elkins's daughter and Adler's niece) and David Boyd (Elkins's grandson) invited Walker (a nonagenarian at the time), whom they both knew, and me to dinner at their home in Hillsborough, California during the late 1990s. Katie and David, who have devotedly supported me through each of my book projects and have been like family to me, felt that Walker would be helpful to my research and would also enlighten me and my passionate interest in interior design. Their prescience and gracious invitation enabled me to talk uninterrupted (except when eating the great hors d'oeuvres we were served) to Walker in the library of their home for almost two hours before we all sat down to dinner, where the conversation about the history of interior design continued throughout the meal.

Walker knew Elkins and personally oversaw several magazine features of her work during her tenure with House & Garden and Vogue. She commended my interest in Adler and Elkins, and discussed their revered contributions to twentieth-century design with me. Walker also spoke about Taylor,

whom she adored and knew well throughout his entire career, and her introduction and voracious promotion of his work to House & Garden and Vogue. Although I was researching Adler and Elkins at the time, I documented everything Walker shared with me about Taylor. It was as if she was grooming me to write a book about him, too.

The quality time I spent with Walker at the Boyds' house was the first of many visits and long-distance telephone conversations Walker and I had over a period of two years. She was energetic, knowledgeable, and extremely supportive of me, my research, and my writing. Unfortunately, Walker died before I completed The Country Houses of David Adler and Frances Elkins. Interior Design.

As with Adler and Elkins, my research on Taylor has been an odyssey. Suzanne Tucker—Taylor's heir apparent—and Timothy Marks, Tucker's husband and managing partner at the San Francisco interior design firm of Tucker and Marks, allowed me absolute access to Taylor's voluminous files and client records, which have been stored since his death in 1986. Suzanne and Tim, along with the members of their staff, also provided their office for my research, always welcoming me as if my needs were their only concern. I am also grateful to Suzanne and Tim for their invaluable memories of Taylor, their introducing me to as many of his clients and associates as possible, and their devoted friendship. Tucker and Marks are to be commended for their fine stewardship of the firm they founded after Taylor's death. He would be proud to see the firm on the AD 100, Architectural Digest's list of the top architects and interior designers whose work appears regularly in the magazine.

Taylor's clients have also enthusiastically encouraged and supported my research. They have respected me and extended complete access to their homes, themselves, and their memories of Taylor, creating quality time for me amid their demanding schedules, and they always treated me as if I was a long-standing friend. They have also expressed their magnanimous appreciation for Taylor, his incomparable talent, and my desire to document it.

I am fortunate to have had access to numerous homes (several that I had photographed for the book) and nonresidential interiors that were decorated by Taylor, as well as many of his clients and their families. They are Dolph and Emily Andrews, Vicki Bagley, Barry and Connie Goodyear Baron, Carolina Barrie, Barbara Beltaire, Lyn Bergeron, Stanley and Lynn Beyer, Roger and Nancy Boas, Barbara Bon, Adair Borba, John and Frances Bowes, Fred and Nina Carroll, Joanna Carson, Lyman and Carol Casey, Emalee Chapman, Warren Clark, Jan Cowles, Douglas Cramer, Delores Dana, Vaughn de Guigne, Charles Evans, Coby Everdell, Liz Familian, Donald and Doris Fisher, Penny Fletcher, Ines Folger, Peter and Barbara Folger, Pat Foster, Gil Garfield, Harvey and Gail Glasser, Jane Glassman, William and Frances Green, Mortimer Hall, William and Candy Hamm, Bob Harmon, Suzanne Haynes, Joseph Hickingbotham, David Hill, Harry and Monica Hunt, Deke and Jeanne Jackson, Michael Jackson, Edward Karkar, Nan Kempner, Thomas Kempner and Anne Bernhard, Nancy Kibbey, Betty Lou Kitto, Pam Kitto, Diana Knowles, Pam Kramlich, Victoria Leonard, Maryon Davies Lewis, David and Bobbie Lundstrom, Bob and Jan MacDonnell, Alicia Martin, Elaine McKeon, Chrissy Merrill, Bailey Meyer, Byron Meyer, Eileen Michael, Bob Miller, Mervin and Roz Morris, Jane Nathanson, Lee Ottserson, Anne Paye, Bob and Alex Phillips, Mary Jane Pool, Peggy Richards, Dorothy Robinson, Helen Rodde, John and Dodie Rosekrans, Ardath Rouas, Claude Rouas, Stanford and Adrienne Rubin, Alexia Ryan, Rita Schreiber, Patsy Seidler, Charles and Edith Seymour, Elisabeth Sherif, Ben Simon, Ned Spieker, Dick and Sue Stephens, Ned and Cathy Topham, Richard Turner, Sandy Walker and Kay Kimpton, Francesca Vietor, Mark Vietor, Noel Vietor, Dede Wilsey, and Sam and Helen Zell.

I thank especially Jeanne Ryan Jackson—Taylor's dear friend and client—who shepherded me throughout San Francisco and arranged, when she was out of town, to have her friends take me everywhere I needed to go in order to see Taylor's work. Jeanne has been a very special and generous friend to me among many wonderful people.

Michael Taylor touched the lives of many people. His friends and professional associates who shared their memories with me include Chuck Arnoldi, Thea Bacon, Stephen Baker, Bernardo and Silvina Barroso, Donzie Barroso, Wilkes Bashford, Bob Bell, Garth Benton, Wade Bentson, Mario Buatta, Dennis Buchner, David Burkholder, Sonja Caproni, George Christy, Charles Cowles, John Crocker, Sam Crocker, John Drum, Barbara Dupont, George Ernston, Lois Esformes, Susan Foslien, Jerry Gere, Richard Gervais, Kathie Gheno, Rene Gregorius, Hester Griffin, Albert Hadley, Denise Hale, Emilio Herraiz, Eddie Holler, Gayle Holmes, Owen Hoyt, Charles Jacobson, Donald and Lillian Jacobson, David Jones, Rod Kagan, Jerrold Lomax, Jim Ludwig, Keith McClelland, Bob Paterson, Stevie Pignatelli, Charles Porter, Chuck Posey, Tom Roberts, Jack Shears, Jeff Smith, Bob Steinwedell, Jack Stephens, John Stewart, Jane Totten, Freddy Victoria, Tony Victoria, Richard Wallace, Paul Weaver, Dennis Westler, Hutton and Ruth Wilkinson, Chuck Williams, Kenneth Winslow, Ruth Winslow, and John Wyninegar.

Michael Taylor. Interior Design is composed of outstanding photo documentation commensurate with Taylor's pioneering interiors. The book revels in the skilled photography of Jaime Ardiles-Arce, Oberto Gili, Steve Haag, Horst P. Horst, Timothy Hursley, Melba Levick, Fred Lyon, Russell MacMasters, Derry Moore, Ezra Stoller, Tim Street-Porter, and John Vaughan, among others. Each of these photographers or their archivists expended great effort and meticulousness in providing the visuals for the book. I also thank Darrin Alfred, Susan Backman, Andre Brandon, Carol Ann Burton, Darryl Cooper, John Eichelberger, Gretchen Fenston, Claire Fortune, Maria Miranda Gresham, James Huntington, Dawn Lucas, Christin Markmann, Leigh Montville, D.Levi Morgan, Cori Park, Linda Santoro, Erica Stoller, Damian Taylor, Layna White, and Warren Wright for facilitating many of the photographs appearing in the book.

I extend my special appreciation to Fred Lyon and Russell MacMasters, both eminent photojournalists and cherished friends of mine, who have unwaveringly guided me throughout the entire process of writing *Michael Taylor. Interior Design*. Fred has been integral to my writing career since "day one," having documented during his illustrious career the work of David Adler, Frances Elkins, and Michael Taylor. I am grateful for his candor, experience, and legendary reminiscences.

I am also fortunate for Russell's support, confidence, and friendship. His insight into Taylor's work and professional life, combined with his own adroitness, brought Taylor to life, making me feel as if I knew him personally. Russell and I have spent hours on end chatting about Taylor, especially during our long weekend visit to Jimmie Wilson's house in Nogales, Arizona, where we melded into the day-to-day lives of Wilson's warm, generous, embracing, and fun-loving niece and nephew-in-law—Bobbie and David Lundstrom, their family, and their friends. Russell's photography of the Wilson commission, taken during our visit, superbly captures interiors of "an era gone by." Russell's career is also legendary, and *Michael Taylor. Interior Design* symbolizes a great deal of his best work.

My family has also been steadfastly supportive throughout each book project. my mother and father, June and Alan Salny, to whom I proudly dedicate *Michael Taylor. Interior Design*; my sister Susan, my brother-in-law Dean Trilling, their two sons, my nephews Scott and Andy; my niece Meghan; my great niece Elsie Rose; my nonagerian grandmother Marion Freedman; and my cousins Judy Corsaro, and Linda and Paul Hershenson, and their families. My late grandparents, Rae Salny Brown, Jacob Freedman, and Samuel Salny, and my late aunts, Barbara Hershenson and Edith Winetsky, also inspired me.

Invaluable editorial guidance, friendship, and support also came from Tristan and Mary Davies. Jessica Friedman shepherded me with sound legal and practical advice. Good friends have also been an important component to this project. Among these are Trudy and Mickey Magarill, who continue to make my life in Baltimore warm, welcoming, and comfortable; Dudley Clendinen, who plays a special role in my life; Robert Caro, Martin Gould, and John Winer, who are long-standing and loyal friends; John Crocker, Faye Florence, Rosemary Cowler, Jack Jarzavek, Eleanor Kress, Janet Ludwig, and Annie Stubbs. Susan Gordon and her son Teddy are special friends, along with Jeff, Lynn, Sara, and Rachel Sachs. I also thank George Everly for his continued support and sound guidance. I appreciate the support and friendship of Bruce Addison, Suzanna Allen, Anthony Barrata, Albert Bartridge, Jane Baum, Thomas Beeton, Wayne and Susan Benjamin, John Berenson, Philip Berger, Ruth Bernstein, Betty Bloomberg, Joe Boccuzzi, Louis Bofferding, Dan Bonnet, Lisa Boudiette, Jim and Diane Bower, Bill and Jori Boyd, Rebecca Bradley, Gert and Kathy Brieger, Bill Brockschmidt, Judy Brown, Joseph Bruce, Michael Bruno, Peter Bruun, Harold Buchbinder, Philip Caggiano, Connie Caplan, Harold Caro, Marilyn Caro, Eric Cohler, Courtney Coleman, Jeff Conti, Patrick Cox, Jack and Peggy Crowe, Jim Dale, John Danzer, Charles de Guigne, Brian Dermitt, John and Missy Derse, David Desmond, William Diamond, Beth Dougherty, Richard Dragisic, Tom and Karen Duffy, Jimmy Duke, Larry Dumont, Louise Duncan, Peter Dunham, Tony Duquette, Douglas Durkin, David Easton, Marilyn Elin, Kaidan Erwin, Kay Evans, Charles Fair, Charles Fair Jr., Rhea Feikin, Bill and Laney Feis, Pat and Cantey Ferchill, Alvan and Lois Finn, Jerry and Betty Fischbein, Beverly Fish, Andrew Fisher, Roy and Joan Flesh, Richard Fowkes, Tully and Elise Friedman, Thomas Fuchs, Melissa Gagen, Steven Gambrel, John Gardiner, Betty Gertz, Grant Gibson, Malin Giddings, Stuart Gilchrist, Joe and Alma Gildenhorn, Joe Gillach, John Gilmer, Jimmy and Shelley Gitomer, Irv and Ginger Gomprecht, Chissa Gordon, Michael and Ellen Gordon, Jared Goss, Michael Graham, Henry and Julie Greene, Leonard and Lois Greenebaum, Stanley and Marjorie Greenebaum, Geoffrey and Maureen Lefton-Greif, Paul Gunther, Ed Gunts, Mark Hampton, Ed Hardy, Henry Harteveldt, John and Carol Hess, Marie Jean, Harry Hinson, Bill Hodgins, Duncan Howard, Alex Jakowec, Charlie Johnston, Eve Kahn, Larry and Evelyn Kamanitz, John Kammeier, Myrna Kaplan, Bob and Marjie Kargman, Spence and Laurie Kass, Alex and Carla Katzenberg, Tom and Diane King, Bill and Dawn Kirsch, Elliott and Fruema Klorfein, Virginia Knowles, Cary and Lisa Kravet, Posy Krehbiel, Fred and Kay Krehbiel, Philip Liederbach, George Livermore, John Lobe, Ed Lobrano, Don Ludwig, Susan Lustik, Robby and Leola Macdonald, John and Carolyn MacKenzie, Jay Marc, Tripp March, Herb and Susan Marcus, Jane Marion, Roth Martin, Connie Martinson, Christopher Mason, Paul Mateyunas, David Maurer, Will McGaul, Phyllis Miller, Bill and Roseanna Milner, Joe Minton, Joe and Diana Monie, David Mordini, Irving and Doris Morris, Keith Morrison, Leonard and Carol Nectow, Karen Nickey, Joe Nye, Liz O'Brien, Mark Olives, Steve Oney, Mitchell Owens, Brandon Pace, William Pahlmann, David Paley, Bret Parsons, Nancy Patz, John and Jane Payne, Kevin Peavy, Jill Petschek, Cameron Polmanteer, Nancy Porter, Scott and Lori Pugatch, Chip Rae, Mark Reader, Peter Reed, Fred and Suzanne Rheinstein, Ralph and Linda Ringler, Ernest Robbins, Rick Robertson, Stan Rodbell, Bonnie Rogers, Sidney and Marilyn Rosenthal, Penny Rozis, Ed and Vicki Rubin, Robert Ruby, Al Ruschmeyer, Marjorie Salter, Mark and Debbie Saran, Gil Schafer, Nick Schloeder, Bobby Schrott, David Seglin, Holly Selby, Andrew and Francoise Skurman, Ellen Small, Britt Smith, Skip Sroka, Dennis and Terry Stanfill, Sherman Starr, Erica Stein, Herb and Renie Stein, Jason Stein, Sharyn Stein, Sheryl Stein, Jimmy Steinmyer, Norman and Norah Stone, Ben Storck, Herbert and Donna Stride, Madeline Stuart, Henrika Taylor, Connie Thompson, Charlotte Triefus, Alice Tucker, Elizabeth Van Ella, Robert Ward, Phyllis Washington, Mike and Jane Weeden, Carol Weis, Jeffry Weisman, Bruce Whipple, Mike and Marilyn Winer, Paul Wiseman, Robert Wrubel, Christian Zanev, Lisa Zebovitz, Susan Zellerbach, and Lloyd Zuckerberg.

I am also appreciative of the following people who helped and supported me during my research for this book. Ida Abelson, Stanley Abercrombie, Christopher Adlington, James Alexander, Michael Allum, Stephanie Angelides, Clarice Baldwin, Thomas Bartlett, Robert Beard, Neil Benezra, John and Gretchen Berggruen, Ralph Bogertman, Lisa Bourquin, Thomas Britt, Wendy Brody, Anthony Bruce, Erica Brunson, Kathy Bryant, Pat Burke, Sam Cardella, Thomas Carey, Evelyn Carr, Jill Carter, Linda Carter, Donna Casey, Kevin Casey, Diane Chapman, Erin Chase, Al and Leslie Cook, Lisa Cregan, Ron Croscetti, Kathy Crowley, Robert Decarlo, Jeanine Docili, Stephen Dudley, Dominick Dunn, Jeffrey Eger, Stephen Elrod, Gwen Evans, Ken Farrar, Lydia Fennett, Melanie Fleischmann, Jody Foor, Tony Freund, Stan Friedman, Tamara Friedman, James Galanos, George Goeggel, Steve Gomez, Charlie Goodyear, Teri Green, Bruce Gregga, Ted and Betty Griffith, Collier Gwin, Pat Hale, Kathleen Harrison, Brent Hartman, Inge Heckel, Henry Hester, Perrietta Hester, Heidi Hickingbotham, Eric Holmgren, Joe Horan, John Irelan, Chippy Irvine, Jay Jeffers, Jean Johnston, Mia Jung, Hilleary Kehrli, Chantal Keller, Jane Kenealy, David Kensington, Margaret Kiekefer, Eleanor Krell, Linda Lake, Michael Lampen, Keith Langham, Gretchen Lawton, Maggie Lidz, Christa McRae, Herman Malvet, Maria Martinez, Kristina May, Alex McClean, Ellen McCluskey, Peter McCoy, Sally McKay, Linda Miller, Margaretta Mitchell, Maureen Mohr, Allison Moore, Carol Morton, Elayne Nathanson, Suzanne Nelms, Jeff Norman, Wendy Owens, William Pahlmann, Jennifer Patton, Becky Phelps, Alix Phillips, Greg and Stacy Renker, Tom Romich, Gayle Rosenberg, Nellie Saliba, Janet Schrim, Jane Schull, Mary Shaw, Rebecca Sherman, Eva Slezak, Michael Stier, Burl Stiff, Tom Stringer, Frances Valesco, Pilar Viladis, Fran Wilson, Matt Wrbican, and Nelly Wuls.

At W. W. Norton, I thank Nancy Green for her continual understanding and support of my passions and my writing; Kevin Olsen, marketing director; Erik Johnson, marketing associate; Vani Kannan, editorial assistant; and Abigail Sturges, designer, whose collaborative input always creates a book with tremendous aesthetic appeal.

LIST OF CLIENTS

SAN FRANCISCO, CALIFORNIA
Mr. and Mrs. Adolphus Andrews Jr., 1957
Mr. and Mrs. Jack Avery
Mr. and Mrs. Robert Bacon, 1982
Dr. Andrew Becker
Ms. Barbara Beltaire, 1982
Mr. and Mrs. Louis Benoist
Mr. and Mrs. Peter Bercut
Mr. and Mrs. Roger Boas, 1976
Mr. and Mrs. John Bowes, 1971
Mr. and Mrs. John Bowes, 1985
Mr. and Mrs. Harry Brawner
Mr. and Mrs. Walter Buck
Mr. and Mrs. Fred Carroll, 1979
Mr. and Mrs. Warren Clark, 1973
Mr. David Dibble, 1968
Mrs. Stanley Dollar Jr, 1982
Mr. Howard Downs, 1984
Mr. and Mrs. Charles Fay Jr, 1958
Mr. and Mrs. Charles Fay Jr, 1966
Mr. and Mrs. Donald Fisher, 1983
Mrs. Ines Folger, 1965
Mr. and Mrs. Peter Folger, 1972
Mr. Vincent Friia
Mr. and Mrs. William Green, 1964
Mr. and Mrs. William Hamm, 1972
Mr. George Hartman
Mr. and Mrs. Elwood Haynes, 1984
Mrs. Diana Hickingbotham, 1967
Mrs. Marion Hill
Mr. and Mrs. Reuben Hills, 1985
Mr. and Mrs. Daniel Jackson, 1958
Mr. and Mrs. Jalson
Mr. and Mrs. Raymond Kassar, 1981
Mr. and Mrs. Gorham Knowles, 1981
Mr. and Mrs. Fred Kohlenberg, 1962
Mr. and Mrs. Richard Kramlich, 1985
Dr. and Mrs. Lloyd Latch, 1977
Mr. and Mrs. Daniel Lewis, 1955
Mr. and Mrs. Daniel Lewis, 1958
Mrs. Maryon Davies Lewis, 1963
Mr. and Mrs. John Maillard, 1983
Mr. and Mrs. Charles Martin, 1950
Ms. Eileen McKeon, 1982
Mr. and Mrs. Steven Merrill, 1974
Mr. Byron Meyer, 1974
Mr. Randy Miller, 1979
Ms. Pat Montandon, 1979
Mr. Herbert Richards, 1955
Mr. and Mrs. John Rosekrans Jr, 1960
Mr. and Mrs. John Rosekrans Jr, 1965
Mr. and Mrs. John Rosekrans Jr, 1980
Mr. and Mrs. Michael Ryan, 1949
Mr. and Mrs. Michael Ryan, 1959
Mr. and Mrs. Michael Ryan, 1961
Mr. and Mrs. Albert Schlesinger, 1957
Mr. and Mrs. Richard Shelton, 1978
Mr. and Mrs. Warren (Ned) Spieker Jr., 1981
Mr. Michael Taylor, 1969
Mr. and Mrs. Paul Temple, 1984
Mr. and Mrs. Brooks Walker, 1958

Mr. and Mrs. John (Sandy) Walker, 1970
Mr. and Mrs. Bercut Waters, 1981
Mrs. Phyllis Wattis, 1977
Mr. and Mrs. Alfred Wilsey, 1982
Mr. and Mrs. Alfred Wilsey, 1984

ATHERTON, CALIFORNIA
Mr. and Mrs. Irving Bartel, 1982
Mr. and Mrs. Donald Fisher, 1976
Mr. and Mrs. Charles Howard, 1962
Mr. and Mrs. Daniel Jackson, 1966
Mr. and Mrs. Mervin Morris, 1970
Mr. and Mrs. John Paye, 1978
Mr. and Mrs. Theodore Rooney, 1975
Mr. and Mrs. Albert Schlesinger, 1958
Mr. and Mrs. Jack Shepard

BURLINGAME, CALIFORNIA
Mr. and Mrs. Robert Avery, 1963

HILLSBOROUGH, CALIFORNIA
Mr. and Mrs. Robert Bacon, 1981
Dr. and Mrs. Stanton Charney
Mr. and Mrs. Thomas Davis, 1954
Mr. and Mrs. Christian de Guigne IV, 1985
Mr. and Mrs. Sterling Edwards, 1951
Mr. and Mrs. William Freer, 1958
Mr. and Mrs. William Freer, 1979
Mr. and Mrs. John Logan, 1957
Mr. and Mrs. John Logan, 1974
Mr. and Mrs. Robert MacDonnell, 1985
Mr. and Mrs. Francis Martin, 1956
Mr. and Mrs. Francis Martin, 1982
Mr. and Mrs. George McKeon, 1973
Mr. and Mrs. Robert Folger Miller Jr, 1969
Mr. and Mrs. Keith Provo
Mr. and Mrs. Charles Seymour, 1975

SAN MATEO, CALIFORNIA
Mr. and Mrs. Jack Foster, 1979

WOODSIDE, CALIFORNIA
Mr. and Mrs. Ralph Davies, 1959
Mr. and Mrs. Charles Fay Jr, 1958
Mr. and Mrs. Paul Fay, 1981
Mr. and Mrs. Herbert Richards, 1957
Mr. and Mrs. William Roberts, 1965
Mr. and Mrs. Michael Ryan, 1960
Mr. and Mrs. Toby Schreiber, 1978
Mr. and Mrs. Peter Wallace, 1982

BOLINAS, CALIFORNIA
Mr. and Mrs. Jack Vietor, 1981

STINSON BEACH, CALIFORNIA
Mr. and Mrs. John Bowes, 1972

NAPA VALLEY, CALIFORNIA
Mr. Francis Ford Coppola, 1978
Ms. Pat Montandon, 1981
Mr. and Mrs. Robert Phillips, 1978

Mr. and Mrs. Toby Schreiber, 1977
Mr. Alfred Wilsey and
Ms. Pat Montandon, 1977

SONOMA, CALIFORNIA
Mrs. Grace Paxton, 1983
Mr. Claude Rouas, 1986

ORINDA, CALIFORNIA
Mr. and Mrs. Clarence Woodard, 1972

PIEDMONT, CALIFORNIA
Mrs. Roberta Ousterman, 1980

PLEASANTON, CALIFORNIA
Dr. and Mrs. Ralph Juhl

TIBURON, CALIFORNIA
Mr. and Mrs. John Huntington, 1984

ROSS, CALIFORNIA
Mr. and Mrs. David Fasken, 1984

LODI, CALIFORNIA
Mr. and Mrs. Duff Chapman, 1951

STOCKTON, CALIFORNIA
Mr. and Mrs. Herbert Kitto, 1950

MODESTO, CALIFORNIA
Mr. and Mrs. Everett Turner, 1956
Mr. and Mrs. Fred Vogel, 1982

MERCED, CALIFORNIA
Mr. George Bianchi, 1985

FAIR OAKS, CALIFORNIA
Mr. and Mrs. Vernon Jones, 1976

COLUSA, CALIFORNIA
Mr. and Mrs. Lee Otterson

LAKE TAHOE, CALIFORNIA
Mr. and Mrs. Gorham Knowles, 1983
Mr. and Mrs. John Paye, 1985

LOS GATOS, CALIFORNIA
Mr. and Mrs. Louis Benoist, 1958

SAN JOSE, CALIFORNIA
Mr. Alex Hirsch, 1981
Mr. Carl Kropf, 1980

ALTA VISTA, CALIFORNIA
Mr. and Mrs. Louis Benoist, 1968

APTOS BEACH, CALIFORNIA
Mr. and Mrs. Louis Benoist
Mr. and Mrs. Charles Fay Jr, 1967

BIG SUR, CALIFORNIA
Mr. and Mrs. Everett Banfield

CARMEL, CALIFORNIA
Mr. and Mrs. Jack Foster, 1980

CARMEL VALLEY, CALIFORNIA
Mr. and Mrs. H. Westinghouse Fletcher, 1952

PEBBLE BEACH, CALIFORNIA
Mr. and Mrs. Paul Avery, 1967
Mr. and Mrs. William Coats, 1960
Mr. and Mrs. H. Westinghouse Fletcher, 1957
Mr. and Mrs. H. Westinghouse Fletcher, 1960
Mr. and Mrs. H. Westinghouse Fletcher, 1963
Mr. and Mrs. Gorham Knowles, 1971
Mr. and Mrs. DeWitt Rucker, 1963

LOS ANGELES, CALIFORNIA
Mr. and Mrs. Stanley Beyer, 1966
Mr. and Mrs. Stanley Beyer, 1975
Mr. and Mrs. Stanley Beyer, 1978
Mr. and Mrs. Stanley Beyer, 1982
Mr. and Mrs. Stanley Beyer, 1985
Mr. Donald Bren, 1974
Mr. and Mrs. Gary Familian, 1971
Mr. and Mrs. Gary Familian, 1978
Mr. Gil Garfield, 1976
Mr. Gil Garfield, 1983
Dr. and Mrs. Harry Glassman, 1979
Mr. Mortimer Hall and
Ms. Diana Lynn, 1963
Mr. Stanley Kramer
Mr. Steve Martin
Mr. and Mrs. Jerry Moss, 1981
Mr. and Mrs. Marc Nathanson, 1978
Mr. Norman Pattiz
Mrs. Violet Rosenberg
Mr. and Mrs. Stanford Rubin, 1976
Mr. Khalid Shawaf, 1982
Mr. and Mrs. Joseph Smith
Mr. and Mrs. Ned Topham, 1983
Mr. James Wilson, 1974

MALIBU, CALIFORNIA
Mr. and Mrs. Stanley Beyer, 1971
Mr. and Mrs. Gary Familian, 1980
Mr. David Geffen, 1982
Mr. Norton Simon and
Ms. Jennifer Jones, 1976

SANTA MONICA, CALIFORNIA
Mr. and Mrs. George Barrie, 1953
Mr. and Mrs. George Barrie, 1957

VENICE BEACH, CALIFORNIA
Mr. and Mrs. Gary Familian, 1975

SANTA YNEZ VALLEY, CALIFORNIA
Mr. Douglas Cramer, 1980

RANCHO SANTA FE, CALIFORNIA
Mr. and Mrs. Allan Simon, 1983
Mr. Raymond Watt and
Mr. and Mrs. Don McMillian, 1981

LA JOLLA, CALIFORNIA
Mr. and Mrs. Jack Vietor, 1981

INDIAN WELLS AND PALM DESERT, CALIFORNIA
Mr. and Mrs. Louis Benoist
Mr. and Mrs. Richard Cramer, 1984

NOGALES, ARIZONA
Mrs. Esther Wilson and
Mr. James Wilson, 1965

BAMOA, MEXICO
Mrs. Esther Wilson, 1974

SUN VALLEY, IDAHO
Mr. and Mrs. Gary Familian, 1981
Mr. Peter Huang, 1981

NETARTS BAY, OREGON
Mr. and Mrs. William Coats

NEW YORK, NEW YORK
Mr. and Mrs. Johnny Carson, 1980
Mr. Charles Evans, 1980
Mr. David Geffen, 1983
Ms. Jacqueline Head, 1983
Mr. and Mrs. Daniel Jackson, 1956
Mr. and Mrs. Thomas Kempner, 1956
Ms. Mary Jane Pool, 1980
Mr. Jules Rosen, 1983
Ms. Linley Sanchez-Elia, 1981
Dr. Gordon Sze, 1981

SOUTHAMPTON, NEW YORK
Ms. Linley Sanchez-Elia

WESTPORT, CONNECTICUT
Dr. Robert Marshall, 1980

WASHINGTON, DISTRICT OF COLUMBIA
Mr. and Mrs. Smith Bagley, 1977

MIAMI BEACH, FLORIDA
Mr. and Mrs. Gardner Cowles, 1953

BOCA GRANDE, FLORIDA
Ms. Linley Sanchez-Elia

ST. PAUL DE VENCE, FRANCE
Mr. and Mrs. Stanley Beyer, 1984

TOKYO, JAPAN
Mr. Mohammed Jameel, 1984

JEDDAH, SAUDI ARABIA
Mr. Mohammed Jameel, 1982

PUBLIC AND COMMERCIAL COMMISSIONS
American President's Line, 1956
Auberge du Soleil
Napa Valley, California, 1980
Auberge du Soleil
Napa Valley, California, 1984
Baker Furniture Company
"New World" group of furniture, 1953
Baker Furniture Company
"Far East Collection," 1955
Burlingame Country Club
Burlingame, California
California Culinary Institute
San Francisco, California, 1985
Decathlon Club
Santa Clara, California, 1984
Elizabeth Arden
San Francisco, California
Fleur de Lys
San Francisco, California, 1970
Hippopotamus Hamburger Restaurant
Menlo Park, California, 1964
Kiahuna Golf Village
Kauai, Hawaii, 1984
Kransco
San Francisco, California, 1984
L'Etoile
San Francisco, California, 1966
Lodge at Pebble Beach
Pebble Beach, California, 1983
Menlo Circus Club
Atherton, California, 1982
PennCorp Financial
Santa Monica, California, 1976
Penncorp Associates
Beverly Hills, California, 1978
PennCorp Financial
New York, New York, 1979
Pennzoil
Houston, Texas
Ralph Lauren Western Wear Showroom
New York, New York, 1980
Specialty Brands
San Francisco, California, 1980
Squaw Valley Lodge
Squaw Valley, California
The Summitt
San Francisco, California, 1973
Texas Club
Dallas, Texas, 1985
Trader Vic's
San Francisco, California, 1962
UNICEF
San Francisco, California, 1980
USS United States

INDEX

PHOTO CREDITS